"Dr. Carson effectively mixes her personal experiences and sensitive reflections as a grandparent with well-formulated wisdom drawn from her clinical work. The result is a uniquely warmhearted, informative and helpful message to all grandparents."

Saul Brown, M.D.
director emeritus, Department of Psychiatry, Cedars Sinai Medical Center
clinical professor of psychiatry, Southern California Psychoanalytic Institute
supervising psychoanalyst, Southern California Psychoanalytic Institute

"Thoughtful, insightful, inspirational—Dr. Carson has given us all a great gift. Give it to your grandparents. Give it to your parents. Give it to your children, and keep one copy for yourself. Loving help has arrived."

Gary David Goldberg
creator and producer, *Family Ties* and *Brooklyn Bridge*

"*The Essential Grandparent* goes to the soul of grandparenting. It celebrates this time in life by connecting the vital spirit of the grandparent to the essence of their tasks. This is a practical book for the entire family."

Jack Canfield
coauthor, *Chicken Soup for the Soul* series

"*The Essential Grandparent* is a must-read book for grandparents of all ages and walks of life. It is a warm, personal and down-to-earth exploration of the years after parenthood that acknowledges the joys and difficulties of the next stage of being. The separating and coming together of new and mature generations can be productive, exciting and challenging. Dr. Carson uses her extensive knowledge and experience to help us understand and integrate our own situations so that we can truly make a difference for our grandchildren, our children and ourselves."

June Sale, M.S.W.
former director, Child Care Services, UCLA
editor, UCLA's *Working Parents Newsletter*
coauthor, *Guide for Working Parents*

"As more of us live longer and as more older people expect and prepare to be active participants in their families and communities, *The Essential Grandparent* comes on the scene at the right time and in the right way. Historically, *The Essential Grandparent* also fulfills the needs of the increasing number of children growing up in single-parent households. The convergence of longer active-adult lives and the fragmentation of immediate-family experiences for children makes it clear that Dr. Lillian Carson's well-written, eminently readable book is essential reading for those who are or will be the grandparents to our children. It advances our capacity as a society to provide children with better continuities and more promising priorities."

Albert J. Solnit, M.D.
Yale Child Study Center
Sterling Professor Emeritus Pediatrics and Psychiatry, Yale University
senior research scientist and commissioner of Mental Health and Addiction Services,
State of Connecticut

"Grandparents are big-time in this era—and here is a fine 'how-to-do-it' book."

Robert N. Butler, M.D.
professor of geriatrics, Mt. Sinai Medical Center, New York
director, International Longevity Center

"One afternoon at Lillian Carson's home, she showed me and a few other guests a costume she was making for a granddaughter: white suede trimmed in vividly brilliant colors, Native-American style. She is no casual grandparent, I thought; she loves, she cares.

"How good it is to read her perceptions of the bonds that can embrace the generations: 'Opening ourselves to the wonder of our child's world. By getting in touch with our "child within" we can free ourselves and our imagination.' There are dos and don'ts, all wisely considered. Overall there is the love, the caring, that makes this book an affirmation of life."

Fay Wray
actress

"What a timely book for present and future grandparents and other interested adults. Sensitive, insightful, informative and meaningful, the author has captured what grandparenthood is all about. Read, enjoy and learn."

Docia Zavitkovsky
past president, National Association for the Education of Young Children

"*The Essential Grandparent* should be essential reading for grandparents and parents, too: both will gain from Dr. Carson's useful advice and wise insights. But the real beneficiaries are children, who will grow richer from a close and loving bond with their grandmas and papas."

Pamela Abrams
editor in chief, *Child Magazine*

THE
ESSENTIAL
GRANDPARENT™

A GUIDE TO
MAKING A DIFFERENCE

DR. LILLIAN CARSON

Health Communications, Inc.
Deerfield Beach, Florida

www.bcibooks.com

We would like to acknowledge the following publishers and individuals for permission to reprint the listed material.

Material from *Terms of Endearment*. Reprinted with permission of Simon & Schuster from TERMS OF ENDEARMENT by Larry McMurtry. ©1975, 1989 by Larry McMurtry. ©1983 by Paramount Pictures Corporation.

Material from *A Woman of Independent Means*, Dell Publishing Co., by Elizabeth Forsythe Hailey ©1979, reprinted by permission of Elizabeth Forsythe Hailey.

"Cathy's Birth" excerpted from *Blueberry Winter: My Earlier Years*, by Margaret Mead, ©1972. William Morrow.

Material excerpted from *Kareem*. Reprinted from *Kareem* by permission of Random House. ©1993 Kareem Abdul-Jabbar.

Words Every Child Must Hear by Cynthia Good ©1994. Reprinted by permission of Longstreet Press.

"What Will We Pass On to Our Children." Reprinted with permission from *Parade*, ©1995.

Excerpted from CHILDREN LEARN WHAT THEY LIVE. Poem Copyright ©1998 by Dorothy Law Nolte. Used by permission of Workman Publishing Co., Inc. New York. All Rights Reserved.

Life Cycle Chart. From CHILDHOOD AND SOCIETY by Erik H. Erikson. Copyright 1950. ©1963 by W.W. Norton & Company, Inc., renewed ©1978, 1991 by Erik H. Erikson. Reprinted by permission of W.W. Norton & Company, Inc.

"101 Ways to Make Your Child Feel Special." Reprinted from *101 Ways to Make Your Child Feel Special*, by Vicky Lansky ©1991. Used with permission of Contemporary Books, Inc., Chicago.

"The Contemporary Family—It's a Classic Plight" by Anne Norberg. Reprinted by permission of Anne Norberg.

"The 8 x 10 photograph . . ." From THE MEASURE OF OUR SUCCESS by Marian Wright Edelman. ©1992 by Marian Wright Edelman. Reprinted by permission of Beacon Press, Boston.

Library of Congress Cataloging-in-Publication Data

Carson, Lillian
    The essential grandparent : a guide for making a difference / Lillian Carson.
       p.   cm.
    Includes bibliographical references and index.
    ISBN-13: 978-1-55874-397-7 (trade paper)
    ISBN-10: 1-55874-397-9 (trade paper)
    1. Grandparenting.   2. Grandparents.   3. Grandparent and child.   I. Title
HQ759.9.C35   1996
649'.1—dc20   96-10421
                                                 CIP

"Essential Grandparent" and the logo are trademarks and service marks of Dr. Lillian Carson.

HCI, its logos and marks are trademarks of Health Communications, Inc.

Publisher: Health Communications, Inc.
             3201 S.W. 15th Street
             Deerfield Beach, Florida 33442-8190

Photo collage design by Lily Guild. Author photo by Joyce Sipple.

To my parents, Gramma Redhair
and Grampa Joe, who set the standard. . . .
And to my family who made it possible.

Contents

Acknowledgments

It takes a family to write a book on grandparenting—from kin to a community of caring friends and colleagues. I could not have done it without the many who offered support and encouragement, sometimes with notes, articles, books and calls, spurring me onward. Those who spoke to me of their experiences, told their stories and shared their wit and wisdom will find their thoughts woven throughout the book. Others read, critiqued and offered ideas. You know who you are. To say I am grateful to each of you is an understatement.

As I travel on this new path of book writing, I have been stretched in many directions. Although now, on the eve of publication, I am surrounded by many who have come to share my vision, it has often been a lonely pursuit. There are some I must name who were pivotal.

David Gershenson has believed from the beginning, encouraging me to keep going, advising me and then miraculously becoming a part of the process. My dear friend Vicki Riskin led the way with her own new writing career and has a way of making me believe in myself. David Rintel's call with praise from Boston gave me confidence beyond measure, and he is a steady ally. Gary David Goldberg has always shared his energy and Diana Meehan calmed my fears.

Sara Miller McCune, a genuine book maven, took me under her wing willingly and with generosity. Mignon McCarthy taught me how to deepen my thoughts and brought organization out of chaos. My dear daughter Carrie somehow made the time to use her artistic skills and provide the attractive, readable presentation that got me started.

The Group—Jean Anderson, Laurie Becklund, Betty Sheinbaum, Gloria Nagy, Vicki Riskin, Karen Sinsheimer and Grace Willens—seems to possess an endless supply of support and encouragement.

Peter Vegso at Health Communications understood that grandparents were viable and caught the vision. Christine Belleris, so easy and steady under pressure, was always responsive. Kim Weiss has rallied behind this project along with the entire organization to meet an impossible deadline.

I appreciate Arielle Ford, along with Shelley Miller, for embracing the message and helping to spread the word; Lily Guild who is even lovelier than her beautiful designs; Judith Williams, who willingly interrupted her life to organize the final stages of production with calm efficiency and care; Phyllis de Picciotto and Leonie de Picciotto who astounded me with the gift of themselves; and Brooke Halpin and Traci Barmen who continue to herald my mission.

The solidarity of my family is my greatest blessing; their patience, love and support cushion my life. And my dear Sam, who I am convinced was sent by my guardian angel, makes each day a celebration. He has been with me every step of the way and is very much a part of this book.

Throughout life's challenges I have always considered myself extraordinarily lucky. This is further proof.

Introduction

I knew becoming a grandparent was possible,
I just couldn't imagine it.

Ready or Not

Ready or not, you're a grandparent! How did you get here so fast? Can it be that just yesterday you were a grandkid yourself and now you're a grandparent? No one consults you about this new role. It is handed to you without your advice or consent. So now that you're here, at this new stage of life, the question before you is, "What are you going to make of it?"

I hope this book will help you find your answer and will assist you in developing a plan for your grandparenting. This is a book for you, about your own hopes, dreams, concerns and conundrums as a grandparent. It will dispel the myths and "tell it like it is." You will learn that other grandparents feel just as you do. It will guide you to become aware of the possibilities, encourage you to trust your intuition, and teach you how to set goals so that you can make the most of this essential role. Just as babies don't come with instructions for parents, they certainly don't come with instructions for grandparents. Being a grandparent has the added complexity that more people are involved and you are not in charge.

First of all, I'm eager that you understand how essential you are to your family. It is your place, at the head of the family, to exercise the wisdom you have acquired. Through life experience, you've learned to set priorities and have developed a philosophy of life. Now you are in a special position to pass this on and shape your grandchildren's lives. You are your grandchild's philosophy teacher, teaching and modeling by your attitudes and actions.

Once upon a time grandparents were respected as the family experts in child-rearing. They were relied upon for their experience and wisdom. But times have changed, and grandparents have been replaced by experts with scientific theories. Today's family has changed, and there is growing concern for the well-being of our grandchildren and their parents. More families face financial difficulties or uncertainty than twenty years ago. More children than ever before grow up without the support and consistent presence of a father in their lives. At any given time, one-quarter of American children are living with just one parent, usually a divorced or never-married mother. For many of these children, their father's physical absence from the home has enormous emotional and financial consequences. Mothers today are more likely than not employed outside the home, their children cared for by others. As both mothers and fathers work longer hours to support their families and advance their careers, children receive less attention and family time. Maintaining the routines of family life—dinner together, family outings, parental participation in their children's school and extracurricular activities—is challenged by work demands and other time constraints. Parents are just plain exhausted. For many, time with their children is difficult to find. Television has replaced conversation and the bedtime story.

I wrote this book to tell you how essential you are and that you have an opportunity to influence the future by your grandparenting.

There are few old-fashioned families with stay-at-home moms, and there is more stress due to divorce and single parenting, interfaith and intercultural marriages, the alternative lifestyles of gay and lesbian parents, and blended families created by remarriage. Overworked parents are overwhelmed by daily demands and are socially isolated. Drugs, crime and the lack of safety, even in our schools, contribute to family anxiety. *There is a crisis in family life and of family values.*

All of this complicates grandparenting. We stand on a new frontier, confronted by unfamiliar situations and uncharted ground. It means we are needed more than ever before. The only cure for family breakdown is family. Our work is cut out for us.

My experience as a psychotherapist, grandmother and grand-daughter has given me respect for the crucial role grandparents play in the lives of their grandchildren. I have listened as my patients have cried out, longing *Recognize the value of genera-* for the comfort and safe haven of their grand- *tional continuity.* parents. I have observed firsthand how young parents rely on the nurture, support and connectedness of their family, and I have enjoyed that special grandparent-grandchild bond.

So many of my patients and others I've interviewed, grown men and women, have passionately declared, *"I would never have made it without my grandparents."* All speak with emotion and gratitude when telling their stories—stories of acceptance and love, of feeling special, of being introduced to new possibilities and encouraged to "go for it." Often these stories are of simple moments, but all attribute "making it in life" to a grandparent. Did you know you could make such a difference? You have the power to change lives! It is these stories that first inspired me to write this book.

I have often wished for reassurance about my feelings and experiences, some bit of encouragement or a reminder that I am not alone on this new frontier. But little has come my way. Even the fact of becoming a grandparent, a major event in the life cycle, has no ritual of celebration, no rite of passage to honor it. What we do receive are questions, not about us but about the new grandbaby and new parents. People don't really talk to us about our experience. We are not asked how becoming a grand-parent affects our lives or changes our view of ourselves. As a result, we are left with many unexpressed feelings about the meaning of this profound passage, feelings that go unexplored. We must digest them on our own.

The title of this book, *The Essential Grandparent,* comes from my belief that as a grandparent you are in a unique position to make a major difference in your grandchildren's lives, and that by doing so, you will open a door to personal fulfillment and successful aging. Active grandparenting is as essential to grandparents as it is to their families. It is not an accident that when I became a grandparent and became aware of its complexities, I found few role models. My own '50s generation grew up at a time when life seemed simple, for we didn't delve beneath the surface. Families lived in closer geographic proximity to each other, and grandparents had prescribed roles. Today, a grandparent's experience is quite different. We need to learn about it. Although we share many common experiences, we all have our own style. Here, in *The Essential Grandparent,* you will encounter many ideas and stories that both validate and add to your experience. They will stimulate your creativity, engender questions, suggest answers and stir excitement. Let this book serve as a catalyst for making a difference. It will encourage and support you and challenge you to grow.

Grandparents are not what they used to be, or at least not what we thought they were.

The joys of grandparenting are available to all. It is healthy for us, the older generation, to nurture the young. It is our natural task to influence the future in this way. There are no requirements for a grandparent to be of a certain color, educational level, lifestyle or economic class. However, just loving our children and grandchildren is not enough. The joy arises from ingenuity, energy and the determination to provide stability and purpose. It is ours for the doing.

My children, like yours, have grown up in a very different world from that of my childhood, with a barrage of competing messages and values.
MARIAN WRIGHT EDELMAN

Joy shared is doubled—
Sorrow shared is cut in half.

My own grandparenthood has stirred the range of my emotions, with all the feelings that accompany relationships. I have experienced my greatest of joys when holding an infant grandchild; or watching two-year-old Harrison, grinning with sheer delight, appear around the turn of the twisting slide; or while trying to hold back my tears as seven-year-old Caitie led her class into the horse-show arena with the confidence of a pro. These are the moments that wipe away doubts. At these moments I am assured that life is good, that the future is promising. But there are other times—times of frustration when I bite my tongue trying not to criticize my daughter when, in my opinion, she disciplines too harshly or when I discover that the TV is on incessantly at my son's.

And there are the worries. All kinds. Worries about health and safety or how relationships are faring. Worries about the world my grandchildren will inherit. Sadness creeps in as I witness the stressed-out lives of these young families and their struggle to keep up.

The advent of grandparenthood stirs up all kinds of memories and images from the past. I remember my own grandparents, who seemed very old and uncommunicative. Their Eastern European world did not seem to translate to mine. My own parents, on the other hand, were ever ready and available to help out and totally involved with my three children. My mother once told me, "I don't know what I would have done without my grandchildren." They became her life. She and my dad were completely devoted. I am caught between extremes. I shall never measure up to the standard of involvement set by my own parents, and the emotional distance of my grandparents is unacceptable. Many of us are in need of new models. The world has changed so rapidly. Grandparents and family life have changed. Both are *endangered species*.

It is possible to change without growing, but it is not possible to grow without changing.
JAMES MILLER

There's another side to becoming a grandparent that most of us don't talk about. It's the age thing. What comes to mind when you hear the word *grandparent*? The stereotypical picture of grandparents who are old? Old and gray and sitting in their rocking chairs? Not vital people leading active lives, and certainly not sexy. It just does not apply to most of us. In fact, I've found some grandparents who find this stereotype so off the mark they don't even want to be called grandma or grandpa. Today's grandparents have broken the mold. We are younger by virtue of health and lifestyle and older because we're living longer.

We grandparents talk a lot about our grandchildren and their parents, our children. We may praise, marvel or complain about them, but we really don't talk about ourselves and the problems and dilemmas we encounter. We leave ourselves out. For example, we really don't talk about how it feels to become a grandparent. I mean how it really feels as the realization dawns that we have moved into a new stage of life as the oldest—or almost the oldest—generation in the family. How it's a sobering reminder of our own mortality combined with the awesome recognition that through our grandchildren, our lives are extended into a future we shall never see. I've found myself wondering about the world my grandchildren will inherit. I wonder how much I will live to see. Will I see my first granddaughter, Caitlin, graduate from college, get married, become a mother? These thoughts of anticipation for future events are coupled with a sense of urgency. I want to be certain to make a difference and leave a worthy legacy.

What's done to children, they will do to society.
KARL MENNINGER

Facts on Families

The family is the single most important social unit for child-rearing and nurturance, and it is continuously changing as it adapts to its environment. It is clear that the well-being of children in this country has been diminishing for at least the past two decades.

In the United States in 1990, 1.7 million new families were created with the birth of a first child. Forty-five percent of these new families had a mother who was either not married, less than twenty years old, or had less than a high-school education. These are families at risk, and their children will be at risk during their critical periods of growth and development. Two strategic age groups have been identified for intervention with preventive measures:

Three million children in the United States live with grandparents.

1. early childhood, while children are still impressionable and responsive to adults;
2. early adolescence (ages ten through fifteen).

Older adolescents are struggling with major biological changes that make it more difficult to change behavior, motivation and the socialization process.

These facts demonstrate how the American family has changed:
- 63.6 million children under the age of 18
  10.4 million are living with a female head of household
  45.3 million (71%) are living with a married couple
  4+% are not living with either parent
- 60% of women whose youngest child is less than six years are in the labor force
- 75% of women with children between the ages of six and 17 years are in the labor force
- 21% of all the children in this country are living in poverty
  45% of African-American children
  40% of Hispanic children
- 68.7% of this country's youth graduate high school
  73.4% of Caucasian youth
  60.7% of African-American youth
  41.6% of Hispanic youth

1

On Becoming a Grandparent

I thought I had my life organized. Then I became a grandparent.

The Things Nobody Talks About

My first thought when my daughter told me she was expecting my first grandchild was, *Oh no, someone else for me to take care of.* I was dismayed by this ungrandmotherly thought, but there it was. Not that I didn't want to be a grandma, but the timing was not what I would have planned.

My daughter, Carrie, and her husband were newly married and not yet established in careers. I was enjoying the relative freedom of having grown children, up and out and living their own lives, especially enjoying it because of my strong sense of responsibility for others, an attribute I ascribe largely to my being a first child. Now, like it or not, I was handed a new caretaking responsibility with a new set of demands. Besides, grandmothers were old, not like me. I was fifty-three, with a busy career and a joyful, new marriage after my widowhood at age fifty. But now, ready or not, I had a new role. I kept my thoughts to myself. It doesn't matter if you are eager for this new role or a bit wary, it happens anyway.

1

We have no choice in our grandparenthood, even though it profoundly affects the rest of our lives. We're accustomed to having some measure of control and choice over matters that affect our lives. We choose our careers, our spouses and where we'll live. We have the option of parenthood, but our grandparenthood is not up to us.

For some, this happy event may come too soon or too late. When grandparenthood arrives early in your thirties or forties, it does not coincide with the expected timetable and can be jarring. You are pushed into a senior role prematurely. A grandchild arriving when you're in your seventies or eighties will challenge your physical stamina, limiting your energy for active involvement. Others may find that the baby's arrival complicates their life by giving rise to new, nagging worries, concerns about the health of the new parents and child, financial problems, the stability of the parents' relationship or how they're raising the child.

When told of her married daughter Emma's pregnancy, Aurora's lip began to tremble. "Emma, it's not the point . . . you shouldn't have . . . ," she said, suddenly on the verge of tears. "What's the point then?" Emma said. "Mee!" Aurora cried. "Don't you see? My life is not settled. Me! Who will I ever . . . get now? What man would want a grandmother? If you could . . . have waited . . . then I might have . . . got somebody."

Later Emma said to her mother, "You're not going to lose your suitors." Aurora's expression was once again a little bemused. "I'm not sure that's why I cried. The shock may have made me jealous, for all I know. I always meant to have more children myself. . . . "

TERMS OF ENDEARMENT, LARRY MCMURTRY

The Age Thing

Some new grandparents may be surprised by sadness or depression, for the advent of grandparenthood confronts them with their own aging. Becoming a grandparent is one more of life's events that wakes us up to our age and where we are on the continuum of life. Like it or not, it moves us along and makes us aware that we are advancing on life's journey. It is a sobering reminder that we are, or are almost, part of the oldest surviving generation. We can number our remaining years. This usually gives rise to a review of our lives, our successes and failures. Take this as an opportunity to rethink priorities. What is worth doing in our remaining years? Grandparenting should rank high on the list.

> Our active lives may defy the stereotypical images of the gray-haired grandparent in a rocking chair, but our new status is still a shock. It's an assault to our self-image, like finding our first gray hair or being offered the senior discount.

I'll never forget the first time a salesperson at a Danish bakery in Solvang interrupted my reverie over the chocolate delight I was purchasing to inquire if I would like the senior discount. My first thought was, *Oh, I'm not old enough,* but on second thought I figured a discount is a discount, so I gulped and agreed. Feeling young and energetic didn't count. You know, I still can't believe I look like a senior. I actually expect to be challenged to show my ID when I request a senior ticket.

If I had known how much fun grandchildren were, I'd have had them first.

As a psychotherapist, I expect and understand the complexity of the feelings stirred by becoming a grandparent as part of being human. Somehow, though, the mixed feelings of joy and trepidation about something as sacred as grandparenthood can make you feel ashamed and want to keep them to yourself. I urge you not to be afraid to admit these contradictory feelings to yourself. The best way to handle the discomfort or shame of mixed feelings is by accepting them as a normal part of life, not by fearing and burying them. Bring them into the open by talking about them. You are not alone. Other grandparents have these thoughts, too.

In fact, you can be pretty certain your adult children have mixed feelings of their own. At times, your children can't help but feel overwhelmed or trapped by the endless demands of parenthood and wish to escape. By remembering the freedom you relinquished to child raising and the resources you spent to support the family, you will find it easy to understand that some misgivings are natural.

Our life choices are often accompanied by a sense of lost possibilities. Acknowledging and accepting mixed feelings without judgment diminishes their power to interfere with our relationships and allows us to give our love and care freely. We become more comfortable in our new role and gain insight into the feelings of others. Becoming a grandparent is yet another reminder that life is bittersweet.

Crossing the Threshold

As my daughter grew larger, the happy thoughts of grandparenting grew on me. I began to get used to the idea, relishing my fantasies about the baby and thoroughly enjoying my daughter's interest in talking to me about pregnancy and parenthood. Although my trepidation was not completely assuaged, I was excited. With the reality of a new baby on the way, I began knitting a sweater and lingering in baby shops. The clincher was meeting the baby, a healthy little girl who arrived three weeks early while I was out of town. I couldn't return to Los Angeles fast enough. Driving to Santa Barbara, I could hardly contain my excitement as we rushed to the hospital.

There she was, Caitlin Lilly. The Lilly is after me. Carrie, my little girl, was holding her little girl. At that moment I crossed the threshold of grandparenthood, a crossing I'll never forget.

I feel a bit uncertain holding this tiny baby. She looks so fragile. I look for familiar features . . . her mouth, ears, eyes, the shape of her face. Whom does she resemble? Could that be my father's chin? Are those my mother's eyes or, maybe, even mine? It seems easier to think about her looks in terms of others than of myself. Are her long fingers like her father's? Yes.

> *Nobody sees a flower—really—it is so small it takes time—we haven't time—and to see takes time, like to have a friend takes time.*
> GEORGIA O'KEEFFE

Reluctantly I recognize that I must share her with the "other side." They, too, have a claim on her. I feel possessive. She's mine—my grandchild. I'm her grandma. Although she has no idea who I am, she will. I will see to that. In her I see my history carried forward. The experiences of my ancestors are now stored in her, and she doesn't even know it . . . or me. She is the future. She will carry the genetic thread forward, beyond me, beyond my time. This is breath-stopping. It is life, past, present and future all rolled into one six-pound, twelve-ounce person. It is difficult to give words to my feelings. A wave of time and emotion is washing over me. It is heady. I ask myself, "What can I do here? What is my place in her life?" I want to do so much. I want her to have every-thing . . . everything good and beautiful, only kindness and warmth and a pony. Yes, she must have a pony as her mother did. May she be blessed with a strong body and mind in order to savor life, a fine edu-cation, a peaceful world. She will not have to escape the pogroms of Eastern Europe as her great-grandfather, my father, did.

While I think of all I want for her, how I will guard the history she holds, how I will nurture all of the possibilities for the future she possesses, how I will protect her and keep her safe, her father approaches. It is time for her to be fed. An abrupt reminder that she is not mine, that it is not my will or vision that prevails. I must entrust her to them, my daughter and son-in-law, lovely children with no experi-ence. How will they know what to do? They are going to raise this baby? This precious bundle who

> *A single event can awaken within us a stranger totally unknown to us. To live is to be slowly born.*
> ANTOINE DE SAINT-EXUPÉRY

holds the key to continuity in my life, the link to my past and future? How can that be? Is that safe? Smiling, he takes her from me. I smile,

We are such stuff as dreams are made of.
SHAKESPEARE

too, to cover up my sense of loss. She is my link. But she is not mine. I must learn to share. But I will find a way to make my mark. I will put my two cents in. She will know she has a Grandma Lilly. She will have a wonderful life. I am resolved. But how do I do it?

Jack Lemmon commenting on the birth of his first grand-child: "I thought I was in total control. I became insane. I was sure the baby's long fingers meant an absolutely brilliant career as a concert pianist. In the birthing room they were doing Lamaze together. The nurse looked at me and decided she'd better take my blood pressure. It was 195 over 86, which set off an alarm, because it's normally 125 over 70."

How to Do It

Worlds can be found by a child and adult bending down and looking together under the grass stems or at the skittering crabs in a tidal pool.
CATHERINE BATESON

Our role as a parent never ends, but it changes radically. Parenting our children and grandparenting our children's children are not the same. For one thing, our role as a grandparent is not as clearly defined as our parenting role. It's not a daily demand, relieving us of the mundane responsibilities for meals or bedtime, getting to school on time or signed up for Little League. We don't have to answer those incessant questions like, "What should I do?" or, "Do I have to take a bath?" or, "Can I have a sleep-over at Ann's?" The dilemmas inherent in parental decisions around discipline or health or school, to name a few, are not ours. Grandparents have the freedom to choose how much time to devote to the family. Each of us determines the amount of our involvement.

Because the extent of our grandparenting is optional, we must define our own role. That definition shapes our actions and the nature of our involvement. On becoming a grandparent we are immediately faced with such questions as:

- Just how much involvement do we want?
- How much time can we give?
- Will we be there for the birth?
- Will we offer help with the baby?
- How much are we needed?
- What are the needs of the new family?
- Will we baby-sit regularly?
- How do we imagine our relationship with our grandchild?
- What do we want to pass on to this new generation?

How to do it? That is the question. How do grandparents establish close relationships with their grandchildren? How do we contribute to their life experience in ways that make a difference? How do we shift gears from parent to grandparent?

Contrary to the popular myth, grandparenting does not come completely naturally, any more than parenting did. It's not always reliable to count on your instincts. Although tuning in to our gut responses is invaluable in human relationships, doing what comes naturally may not always be best. We need to think before we act. Think about the effect our responses may have on our family relationships and needs. This does not rule out spontaneity. By adopting a thoughtful attitude, however, we will make it more certain that our words and deeds are providing the support that is needed and that they will enhance our relationships. Just a simple comment like, "Oh, her little feet are cold," might be taken as criticism by new parents.

An example of how uncharted grandparenting remains is the call I received from my friend Ethel. She, a take-charge executive, the first female vice-president of a major entertainment corporation, was in a panic. Concerned about her new granddaughter's health, she couldn't figure out how to talk to her son and daughter-in-law in a supportive way without interfering. Here she was, a pro at handling emergencies and solving problems, but grandparenting had her stymied. Her dismay was evident as she wailed, "I thought grandparenting was supposed to come naturally." This is one of the myths that causes us to feel inadequate.

My friend had some legitimate concerns. Her granddaughter was not thriving. Something was wrong. Ethel hesitated to voice her alarm, since she did not want to alienate her children by appearing to be critical. I suggested that she share her concerns with her children. When this is done thoughtfully, without alarm or judgment, it can be helpful. "The baby does seem listless and her appetite is poor. This is cause for concern. I'd check this out with the doctor if I were you." Then, having stated your opinion, leave the rest to the parents. Ethel had the satisfaction of expressing her views. Her manner was low key to avoid upsetting the parents. Actually, her statement was helpful. It validated the parents' concerns and prompted them to action. When we do express our views we must be ready to let go of the outcome. The rest is up to the parents.

After much deliberation, I recently shared my concern that two-and-a-half-year-old Harrison's unusually high activity level might be hyperactivity or ADD (attention deficit disorder), as it is now known. His parents disagreed.

I explained a child's need to focus on activities and complete tasks in order to develop a sense of competence and self-esteem. This is a problem for hyperactive kids. I suggested that Harrison would benefit from special attention in these areas.

Now when I'm told of Harrison's exhausting, nonstop behavior, I am sympathetic, but I do not mention ADD. What purpose would it serve? Whatever it's called, this child is a handful—adorable, loving, smart and exhausting. My input is confined to bringing toys, blocks and books, for example, activities that might capture his attention and help him to focus. I enjoy him and focus on creatively thinking of activities that might occupy him. Water play is a winner. When we're together I try to help him focus and complete activities. I've defined my role as that of supporter and creative influence but clearly not in charge. It's not always easy and, yes, I do worry. The good news? His attention span is growing. Maybe I am wrong.

Grandparenthood is new territory. We have some learning to do. We are not in charge of the parents or the parenting. Our relationship to them has changed. Pitfalls will be avoided by giving thought to the effect of our actions or responses.

The true secret of giving advice is, after you have given it honestly, to be perfectly indifferent whether it is taken or not and never persist in trying to set people right.

JOHN ROSEMOND

Along the way, we grandparents learn the value of exercising an incredible amount of tact. We regularly bite our tongues and zip our lips. Sound like a tall order? You *can* do it. It's just like everything else in life: you reap what you sow. This book is my guarantee that it's absolutely worth it. I offer you my ideas and my encouragement to "go for it."

The Gift

As parents we are offered the experience of two childhoods, our own and that of our children. As grandparents we have a third chance to experience "the first great wonder at the world," childhood's view. This is a gift to us that can be fully received by opening ourselves to its many possibilities.

It takes a long while to grow young.

PABLO PICASSO

Opening ourselves to the wonder of childhood means entering the child's world. By getting in touch with our "child within," we can free ourselves and our imagination. Can we allow ourselves to be playful or silly? Can we stop to take the time to watch the shapes in the clouds and create stories from our mind's eye? Can we nurture our curiosity? To the child, the world is endlessly fascinating.

If a child is to keep his inborn sense of wonder . . . he needs the companionship of at least one adult who can share it, rediscovering with him the joy, excitement and mystery of the world we live in.

RACHEL CARSON

Among the most valuable but least appreciated experiences grandparenthood can provide are the opportunities it offers for exploring, re-living and resolving one's own childhood problems in the context of one's relationship with one's grandchild.

I'll never forget what a little five-year-old patient told me. We

Living is a gift of wonder. Let me share it with my grand-child.

Essentially parenthood is not learned. Parenthood is an inner change.

MR. ROGERS

were enjoying an activity together when I spontaneously exclaimed, "I'm having so much fun!" She looked at me quizzically and responded, "Grownups aren't supposed to have fun." How many of us are bound by this belief? What keeps us from letting go and having fun? Can we shake off the self-imposed restrictions that keep us from joy and wonder?

Two-and-a-half-year-old Harrison wanted to use the camera. He kept saying, "I want to hide." I finally figured out that when I'm taking a photo the camera is in front of my face as if I were hiding. It made perfect sense.

One day as Caitie and I entered the zoo she went running and skipping ahead of me. She turned and called, "Come on, Grandma!" I answered by running and skipping, too. As I skipped, I had a thought of recognition, I remember how I used to do this. For the moment I experienced the sense of freedom and pure joy of my childhood. Caitie and I were sharing an experience that linked us together. Only later did I imagine how silly I must have looked to any onlooker.

Don't Leave Yourself Out

As a psychotherapist working with children and families, my counsel is sought by parents for a variety of their parenting problems. When grandparents see me, often while helping out by bringing their grandchild to an appointment, they will occasionally ask about a problem a grandchild may be having or may tell me of a concern about the parenting they witness. But no grandparent has ever spoken to me without prompting regarding his or her feelings about grandparenting. Yet, as I began talking to grandparents, I discovered that they are so eager to talk about their grandparenting experiences that they don't want to stop.

There are so many questions. It's truly like opening Pandora's box. A grandparent's thoughts, dilemmas and joys often remain unexpressed and unrecognized. In fact, grandparents have a need to talk about their feelings and experiences.

Grandchildren provide an avenue that leads us right into life. With them we experience life unfolding. Their fresh view not only delights us but awakens us to new possibilities. It's refreshing. It's healthy. It keeps us young. It is the joy of grandparenting.

Most grandparents are reluctant to bore friends with personal tales of grandchildren. I think we're also embarrassed by the personal nature of our concerns or complaints when they don't fit our expectations of how grandparents should feel. When we are determined not to be boring, we may make a pact with or among ourselves not to talk about our grandchildren in public. This results in unanswered questions and unexplored experiences. Under these circumstances, grandparenting becomes an isolated experience. Sure, we talk about our children and grandchildren. What we don't talk about is our own feelings.

Talking about our feelings is good for us. In fact, it allows us to let go of the feelings, to put them to rest and move beyond them.

When we're upset or feeling critical of our children, we may suffer a nagging suspicion that there is something wrong with us or our family. One of the advantages a therapist has is knowing that all families have problems. There is no such thing as a perfect family, but the notion of perfection tends to make us keep our thoughts and worries to ourselves.

Celebrate Your Own Experience

When you become a grandparent, nobody talks to you about you. Oh yes, they congratulate you on becoming a grandparent, and then they quickly ask about the baby. Is it a boy or a girl? Did the mother have an easy delivery? How are they doing? Does anyone think to ask how you are doing or feeling? It is expected that you are joyful, which you no doubt are, but the deeper impact of the event is overlooked. The new parents have a lot of needs. The baby requires attention. Do the grandparents also have needs? You bet.

Becoming a grandparent requires preparation on your part, too. You've had to plan your time around the arrival and figure out how much time you can devote to helping out. This means making choices and juggling all your responsibilities and interests at home, at work and in your personal life. No matter how thrilled you are by the coming event, you will be altering your life in order to participate. Mostly it's taken for granted that you'll do that—no big deal, except to you.

Where is it written that you must drop everything to help out? If you do, appreciate how you are giving of yourself and savor some of the satisfaction that brings. For those who don't go to help out early on, don't feel you aren't being good grandparents. Those expectations of what grandparents *should* do produce unnecessary guilt. We have lost the security people once derived from long-standing customs, from growing up as part of an extended family and from the experiences these provided. You have no power over the expectations of others, but you do have the power to take charge of your own. When determining your involvement, respect your own needs. In fact, it's vitally important to your effectiveness in the family to maintain your own life. Making your kids your whole life is unhealthy. Give what is right for you. As important as your support is, over-involvement is not only intrusive, you may also find yourself taken for granted. Resentment creeps into relationships based on meeting the expectations of others.

How much help is enough? In the dynamic relationship of grandparenting, these questions are never answered once and for all. Each situation differs, so rules don't work. Juggling between your own needs and theirs is a continual balancing act. I have adapted psychoanalyst D. W. Winnicott's concept of a *good-enough* parent to that of *good-enough* grandparent. The term *good enough* focuses on your overall effort rather than each individual act. It suggests that in order to grandparent well, one ought not try to be a perfect grandparent, just as one should not expect perfection in others. Perfection is not within the grasp of ordinary human beings. Efforts to attain it typically interfere with that lenient response to the imperfections of others, including those of one's children and grandchildren, which make good human relations possible.

It is quite possible to be a *good-enough* grandparent—that is, a grandparent who grandparents well. When you are not able to be there and guilt sets in, remind yourself of the overall picture and of how you do contribute. Making plans for what you will do in the future is another antidote for guilt.

Although you don't have to do anything to become a grand-parent, if you want to reap its rewards by developing a meaningful relationship with your grandchild, you do have to do something. You must struggle and juggle to make room for it in your life. To form a relationship and make a difference requires time, creative thought, planning and effort.

> *We prefer to invest in build-ings and roads and super-structure and technology, and we have forgotten how to invest in our children.*
>
> JANET RENO

Mark Your Passage

My friend Diana told me a story of how the transition of her mother, Brenda, into grandparenthood was recognized by her mother's friend. When Shana, Diana's first child and the first grandchild was born, the friend arrived with two gifts, one for the new grandma, Brenda, and one for baby Shana. Grandma's gift was much more impressive than the baby's present. Diana was puzzled and a bit miffed. After all, Shana was the main event, the center of attention, and should receive the best gift. This sensitive friend was quick to explain that the grandmother's gift was in recognition of her important passage to grandparenthood. That story impressed me and has inspired me to celebrate the grandparenthood of my friends. I've been giving gifts to new grandparents ever since. It's especially fun because the gifts are totally unexpected.

Some of my favorite gifts for new grandparents:
- *Unbreakable dishes or eating utensils to use for visits*
- *Books to share with grandchildren*
- *Toys to start a grandparent's collection*
- *Tapes, CDs, videos*
- *Tape recorder for storytelling*
- *Picture frame or album*

When we undergo a change uncelebrated and unmarked, that transition is devalued, rendered invisible.

Nowadays, there is a growing recognition of the value of ritual in our lives. Ceremonially marking a significant passage adds dimension to our lives by providing a special time for us to appreciate life, ourselves and each other. It can be a time to reassess where we've been and plan where we are going. Rituals give meaning and purpose to our passages.

Mark your passage into grandparenthood. Create a rite of your own to celebrate your new status. It doesn't matter if it's simple or elaborate or if your grandchildren have already been here for a while. Any ritual is an opportunity for transformation. What matters is that it have meaning for you. It is a way, not only to honor yourself, but to honor the value of family.

Your rite can be anything you want it to be. It can be with you alone, with your spouse, or with others. One couple I know planned a picnic in a lovely place to talk about their feelings about grandparenthood. They reminisced about their own grandparents and how they both envisioned their own role as grandparents now. Together, they planned how to become the grandparents they hoped to be.

Another couple, Ruth and Bill, held a tree-planting ceremony when they became grandparents. Watching their growing tree reminds them of their growing family.

Nanna Tina paid a visit to a church she had always thought especially beautiful. She lit candles for herself and her grandchild and spent a contemplative hour there. A grandmother who writes poetry wrote of her passage and then shared it at a special family dinner.

Several grandparents I know have written extensively in their journals about their thoughts, hopes and dreams of grandparenthood. Grandfather Leonard wrote a letter to his newborn grandson that is destined to become the child's lifelong guide. In it Grandpa Leonard describes his philosophy and his views on a worthwhile life. Grandpa Jim shared his thoughts about his passage in an informal discussion with his men's group. In spite of the variations of the rituals marking their passage, all have reported them deeply gratifying. Perhaps Grandma Grace spoke for all who have employed a ritual to mark their transition to grandparenthood when she said: "I felt a deepened awareness of the purpose of my existence and my connection to past and future through family."

Creating Your Own Rite of Passage

You may do anything that you feel will add value and richness to your life, from the most simple symbolic gesture to an elaborate plan. The only thing that matters is that it has meaning for you, that it celebrates your passage and honors you by elevating your experience above everyday life. Rituals and rites of passage are markers of significant moments. By dignifying our lives, they encourage us to participate in the moment. Let your ritual encourage you to lead a proactive life. When deciding on a ritual of your own, set aside some time to plan. Here are some questions to guide your thoughts. Consider your feelings, the negative as well as the positive. List them along with your responses to these questions:

Rituals reflect your values.

A ritual is a structured sequence of actions that brings us a heightened sense of our own identity and meaningfulness.

- What meaning does grandparenthood have for you?
- List your feelings (the negative as well as the positive).
- What rituals have had meaning for you in the past? Religious rituals? Family rituals? Personal rituals?

- Would you like to adapt any part of them into your grand-parent ritual?
- Do you prefer a private ritual or one with your spouse or with others?
- What activities hold meaning for you?
- What are the new tasks of grandparenthood?

Be creative. Let yourself imagine all sorts of possibilities.

RITUALS

1. Any ritual is an opportunity for trans-formation. To do ritual, you must be willing to be transformed in some way.

2. Ritual affirms the value of any transition.

3. When we undergo a change uncelebrated and unmarked, the transi-tion is devalued and rendered invisible.

4. When we celebrate with others, life changes. Together, we create strong bonds of intimacy and trust that can generate new culture.

5. Ritual that is alive does not become frozen in form.

Ritual in Bali

Each stage of Balinese life is honored with ritual. Lavish offerings, decorations and feasts are prepared; elaborate costumes are donned, and music and laughter shimmer through the air. At the core of all the fes-tivity is an awareness that the purpose of purification and spiritual strengthening is being fulfilled.

Through ceremony, the life cycle unfolds. Through ceremony, the children grow up learning to trust and respect themselves as well. The result is apparent in the adult members of society—in their astonishing grace, their gentle strength and their gen-erosity of spirit.

Changed Relationships

When your children have their own children, a new phase of life begins in your life and theirs. Your attention is turned toward them. Their attention is on their new family. Your kids don't have the time they previously had for you. It's not the same. Even when they come for dinner or you go on an outing together, the baby is there demanding attention. Of course being with the baby is ever fascinating, but their preoccupation with her changes the dynamic between you and may be experienced with a vague sense of disappointment or loss. Even though your support is needed now more than ever, your relationship with your adult children undergoes many changes. They are not able to be as tuned into you or your interests. It's not that they don't care as much but that their focus has changed. If you formerly enjoyed long conversations with them and "hanging out" together shopping, skiing or whatever, it's different now. If time for togetherness was in short supply before the baby, it may be even shorter now. Each step forward in life requires relinquishing some of what has existed before. It is a law of nature that growth necessitates loss. When the infant is weaned to a cup, she gives up that special closeness of being held. We applaud it as growth, but to her and her mother it is also an end to the special closeness of nursing and feels like loss as well. Sadness creeps in even while rejoicing. Acknowledging it helps. Then celebrate.

When we say of a couple, "They are starting a family," we are recognizing that the new unit being formed is made up of its own mix of genes. It is the start of a truly new and unique combination. The arrival of the first child is a watershed event for the parents. The change a baby makes in their lives is often much greater than they anticipated or at first realized. Some parents initially try to go on about their lives just as before, but they soon become aware of how their days are altered. The new external arrangements that caretaking requires mirror important internal changes in the new parents. Parenthood precipitates deep-seated and far-reaching modifications in their views of themselves and of their purpose in life.

As soon as the first baby arrives, there is a shift in the marital relationship. A spouse is no longer seen and experienced only as one's mate, but simultaneously also as the parent of one's child. The situation is not made any easier by the fact that parents often harbor contradictory hopes or values which coexist peacefully beside each other in their fantasies. A mother may wish for a tranquil, accepting baby while at the same time expecting her to have a strong personality with a "mind of her own." One new father told me he was looking forward to active involvement with his new baby although his fast-track job demanded most of his time.

Becoming a parent also subjects one to the reliving—partly consciously but largely unconsciously—of many of one's childhood experiences and problems. It tempts one to try to solve these by doing things differently than their own parents. New parents often tell me, "I'm not going to do it the way my parents did."

It is not possible to anticipate how parenthood changes your life.

If they felt you were too strict a disciplinarian, they will vow to be lenient. If they longed for more of your time, they are determined to be more involved. Parenthood recalls baggage from the past. As some painful experiences or perceived injustices from their own childhood surface, they vow to do better. The trouble, I've observed, is that they're not sure what they should do instead. This uncertainty unexpectedly activates negative feelings toward us and can be the source of tension between the two generations. They are torn between the conflicts from the past and their need for our support. This leads to emotional distancing. You can see why it's risky to jump in with your advice. Waiting to be asked your opinion is frustrating but more effective in the long run. Criticism, even "for their own good," is damaging to your relationship.

I'd say that in terms of life-changing experiences, having a baby at forty-three was greater than winning the Pulitzer.

JANE SMILEY

The mere presence of the child and the necessity of taking care of her forces the parents to deal with these issues; thus living with a child involves much more than reality testing against one's fantasies of how good a parent one might be, how wonderful or troublesome one's child will be, or what kind of a parent one's mate will be. Parenting makes it necessary to measure one's fantasies about what a family can and should be against the everyday reality of family living.

Of course change brings rewards, too. When your kids become parents you are offered new experiences. It's a thrill to see them in their new role. As they seek their new identity as parents, you, too, are finding your way as a grandparent.

Over time, the challenges of parenting begin to soften your child's hurts of the past. She or he develops a new respect for the difficult job of parenting and is more forgiving of your imperfections. This brings an opportunity for dialogue between you on an entirely new plane, because you have something new in common. You're both parents and you're both focused on the welfare of the same person, your grandchild. New understanding and the healing of past grievances then can take place and lead to closer family ties.

I offered to stay with my daughter and help after her first baby was born. She told me her friends had advised that no matter how good your mother might be, a hired nurse is better. I'm so worried that I will be shut out of this baby's life. I just want them to let me love her.

GRANDMA PHYLLIS

One thing all new parents have in common is an abundant need for your support. When we are able to praise our children's parenting efforts, we are filling that need. Find it in your heart to praise even imperfect efforts, remembering that we learn from our mistakes.

Grandma Lynn, who has two infant grandchildren, spoke of her unexpected pleasure watching her daughters as mothers. "It's such a joy to see them in their new role as parents, and I find that I don't have any desire to tell them how to do it. They seem so comfortable with their babies and they're enjoying them so much. I was much more anxious when I was a new mother."

Becoming a grandparent strengthened my relationship with my adult children. They became more interested in family matters.

PAPA SAM

Most of us look with hindsight on our parenting years with some regret about what we might have done differently. Grandparenting allows us to do it again, only better. It gives us a chance to heal.

"I am determined not to repeat with my grandchildren the mistake I made with my children—using every means of coercion at my command, emotional as well as financial, to keep them close to me. Ever since Andrew came home from the war, I have had both children at my beck and call. I try to take comfort in the duty visits they pay once a week, but in my heart I am bereft. Polite strangers have taken the place of the two precious allies I sought to keep at my side forever. No mother was ever more terrified of being abandoned in her old age than I—and no mother ever did more to make it happen by doing so much to prevent it. But at least as consolation for the loss of my children, I have had the good fortune to become my grandchildren's best friend. When September comes, I am determined to bid my namesake bon voyage without a tear as she sets out on a marital adventure that will take her everywhere but back to Texas to live. I wonder where her mother would be today if I had not kept begging her to return home. One life is simply not enough for all the lessons there are to learn. Thank God for grandchildren! I would like my epitaph to read, 'To be continued . . .'"

Je vous embrasse, Bess
A Woman of Independent Means, Elizabeth Hailey

Advice on Advice

Everyone is entitled to my opinion.
Yogi Berra

Having grandchildren gives you more to worry about. The good news is that you don't have the daily work of raising them. The bad news: you are not in charge. You can heave a sigh of relief. It's clear from the beginning that you are not making the decisions. After all, the decision to have a baby wasn't yours to make. This issue of control continues over time. The naming of the baby is a case in point. My husband and I have a strong bias for naming babies after family members. We feel that names reflect a family history and have spiritual meaning. So we subtly and not-so-subtly employed our powers of persuasion.

One day my expectant daughter-in-law dropped by to announce that she had *the* name for a girl. Oh, great, I thought. Naming this unknown little person would provide her with an identity.

"What is it?" I asked eagerly.

"Scarlett," she replied proudly.

"Oh," was all I could say. It was definitely not my style.

"You don't like it," she accused.

This required diplomacy. "First of all, it doesn't matter what I like . . . but," I ventured, "I've always thought that with such a hard-to-pronounce last name, a simple first name is best."

The matter was dropped. The baby was a boy. He wasn't named for my father as I had hoped. His first name has no relation to the family, but his middle name is after his grandfather.

> *What's in a name? that which we call a rose / By any other name would smell as sweet.*
>
> SHAKESPEARE

Their response to our preference has proved to be a pretty good measure of our influence. Our input was considered and then interpreted in their own way. My daughter did just about the same when naming her two daughters. I believe there is a message here. The parents are taking charge. In effect they are saying, "We appreciate your ideas, but we'll do it our way." My admonition to myself and to you: accept it with a smile, remembering that, after all, it's their show. And by all means, keep your disappointment to yourself. There will be many reminders that learning to let go of the in-charge parenting role is a continual challenge.

> *When my son and namesake, Samuel Thomas Hurst V, became a father I anticipated with pride the heritage his son would carry as Samuel Thomas Hurst VI. They named him Nathan, a name without family ties. I keep my disappointment to myself.*

Of course we want our grandchildren to have only the best possible care. We each have opinions and, after all, we do have the advantage of experience. Can we trust these novices with such an important task? Each parent has his own way of doing things, which may not fit our own. There are so many individual parenting styles and customs, so there are bound to be some things that you'd certainly do differently. Perhaps they let the baby cry, and you can't stand it; or maybe they won't let the baby cry, and you're sure they're spoiling her. You are entitled to your point of view, but you are not, I repeat *not*, entitled to meddle. They are in charge, not you. The dilemmas that result from this challenge to accept your secondary position do not go away but continue to complicate your life. When one confronts you, take a deep breath and remember not to make suggestions without being asked. Don't kid yourself by thinking that asking a question really isn't interference. I've done it myself only to realize later that I was not only expressing my concern but suggesting what I'd like them to do. Although it is more tactful to ask, "Do you think you should call the doctor?" it is still a judgment. Even your tone of voice conveys a message. We must earn the right to voice our opinion by establishing a supportive relationship with praise, encouragement and assistance.

> *To be a parent is to have a special "irrational" feeling of responsibility for a special being.*
>
> JAMES GARBARINO

Do we have the right to tamper with another person's self-esteem? Have you ever thought that it works both ways? They may have some suggestions for us, too. Besides, the response to suggestions or criticism is most often defensive and resistant to the idea. So it really doesn't help. Begin a dialogue. Ask for their advice on your grandparent role and what they want or expect of you. By establishing a supportive relationship you can create a climate of collaboration. Provide encouragement by letting them know how well they're doing. Sympathize with their problems. Then they can seek your input without fear of judgment.

> *In the Pueblo world, beauty was manifested in behavior and in one's relationships with other living beings.*
>
> LESLIE MARMON SILKO

Expressing her resolve as a mother, Margaret Mead writes, "I tried to let her be free to choose her own path, and in January, 1947, I wrote—for her—the last poem I have ever written."

CATHY'S BIRTH

That I be not a restless ghost
Who haunts your footsteps as they pass
Beyond the point where you have left
Me standing in the newsprung grass,

You must be free to take a path
Whose end I feel no need to know,
No irking fever to be sure
You went where I would have to go.

Those who would fence the future in
Between two walls of well-laid stones
But lay a ghost walk for themselves,
A dreary walk for dusty bones.

So you can go without regret
Away from this familiar land,
Leaving your kiss upon my hair
And all the future in your hands.

MARGARET MEAD

Grandma Nina told me of her early lesson in holding her thoughts shortly after her first grandson had arrived. In the Jewish tradition there is a Bris, a gathering of family and friends to witness and then celebrate the newborn's circumcision. "My son announced that he was not going to have a traditional Bris. This seemed to be a declaration of independence. I just answered, 'Oh,' hopefully hiding my disappointment and knowing that his father would really be upset. Well, it turned out that the changes they made were not that radical. I was really relieved. It was basically a traditional celebration. I'm so glad I held my tongue and didn't get upset by my son's original statement. It was a good lesson. I

We are formed by the lives which intersect us. The larger and richer our community, the larger and richer is the content of self.

PARKER PALMER

learned that allowing the children's plans to unfold without inter-ference is the best policy."

Between you and your kids the playing field is never level. Your voice remains that of the parent and packs a greater wallop.

No parent or grandparent is immune to uncertainty and guilt regarding childrearing today. The job is a tangle of double binds.

The feeling of wholeness and connection with the past through family is central to human experience.

JAMES GARBARINO

Although it is usually best to keep silent, there are exceptions—times when a situation nearly requires that the grandparent speak up. For example, I recently came upon my two-year-old grandson, Harrison, left alone in the bath-tub by his sitter who was sitting in the kitchen. For me, this was too important a safety issue to go unreported. My daughter-in-law appreci-ated my input. As a rule of thumb, however, we can all listen to the wise grandmother who said, "The reason we are given two ears and one mouth is so we can listen twice as much as we speak."

- Today, 58 million Americans are grandparents.
- 50% of adults ages 45 to 59 and 83% of adults 60 and over are grandparents.
- By the year 2005, there will be more than 76 million grandparents in the United States. Nearly half of all grand-parents will be baby boomers.
- More than 66% of grandparents have at least three grand-children.
- Almost 90% of grandparents take an active interest in their grandchildren.
- More than 66% of grandparents talk to their grandchildren by phone at least once a month.
- More than one-fifth of grandparents take grand-children with them on a trip or to a movie, sporting event or museum at least once a month.
- 44% of grandparents spend 100 or more hours taking care of their grandchildren during the year.

- One-third of grandparents enjoy taking their grandchildren shopping at least once a month.
- 50% of grandparents spend more than $320 annually on gifts for grandchildren.
- In 1992, grandparents spent $8.3 billion on gifts for their grandchildren.

American Demographics (September 1993)
National Institute on Aging: Roper Starch Worldwide

DOs AND DON'Ts

1. DO acknowledge to yourself, and to others if you wish, your mixed feelings about grandparenthood and accept these feelings as deeply human.

2. DO think about the people in your own life who have made a difference and let them serve as role models.

3. DO accept the challenge to experience the wonder of childhood.

4. DO celebrate your passage into grandparenthood with a meaningful ritual, however simple.

5. DO assist others by acknowledging their grandparenthood.

6. DO acknowledge and accept the changes in your relationships with your adult children. These are the inevitable joys and pains of growing.

7. DON'T forget that you're not in charge, that you must let go.

8. DO support your children with praise for their parenting struggles. It will improve your relationship, and they will be more open to your input.

9. DON'T criticize your children or grandchildren.

10. DO remember that relationships are a two-way street.

2

The Essential Grandparent

The Importance of Being a Grandparent

Grandparents and grandchildren have much to tell each other. One has just come from the spirit world and the other is on their way to the spirit world.
TAUTAHCHO, Chumash People

Grandparents and their families are both endangered species. As a grandparent you are more essential to your family than ever before. I wrote this book to tell you why you are needed and of the great opportunity you have been given to influence the future.

Life today is not family-friendly. Once upon a time, family life seemed simple. People got married, had children and raised them without much fuss. Family members lived near each other, moms stayed at home, and grandparents were relied on as a natural part of the family. It's different now. More moms go to work, and more kids go to daycare. The 50 percent divorce rate has reshaped the family into many new configurations. There are many more single-parent families, some headed by dads as well as moms and blended families (his, hers and ours). That means more step-grandparents and step-grandchildren. Because of the increase in interfaith and intercultural marriages, there is more diversity within families. Many gay and lesbian couples are having children. There is also more mobility. Often the physical distance that separates us from our grandchildren weakens our connections. The result is less support available from the extended family.

Faced with the need to juggle the demands of work and home, families have become disconnected from one another and from their communities. More families are socially isolated. All of this has resulted in a crisis for our grandchildren. Their needs are not being met. No one is available to listen to them. How can they develop a sense of purpose in their lives or learn that their lives have meaning? They are starved for attention and a sense of family continuity.

The overcommitted lifestyles of today's parents leave them exhausted and their children unattended. Parents, particularly

The grandparents' job is to give their grandchildren roots and wings.

fathers, are devoting less time to their children. We grandparents have our work cut out for us. We can make a difference. We can listen. We can teach. We can spend the time that shows our grandchildren they are valuable.

Research supports the importance of this message by providing evidence that caring adults make a difference in children's lives. To the puzzling question about what it takes to succeed in life—why it is that some succeed in spite of impossible conditions, while others, even some who are seemingly better off, crumble—we now have an answer. It is a deceptively simple answer, which holds a clear and exciting message. Without exception, those who succeed in the face of great odds describe the presence of a caring adult during their childhood, one who *believed* in them and helped them to *believe* in themselves. This caring adult is often a grandparent. It could be you.

Nurturing our grandchildren has added benefits. It is our natural task to care for the young. Involvement with our grandchildren provides fulfillment as we encounter aspects of ourselves, our partners and our parents in the next generation. There is a special delight when we identify our own characteristics, interests and talents in our grandchildren. "My granddaughter is interested in horses, like me." "The kids are smart, like their grandfather." "She has her mother's passion, that first grandchild of ours. Come to think of it, my mother had that passion, too. And my wife's two grandmothers." By seeking to identify characteristics across several generations, we place ourselves in generational history. We assist the establishment of the next generation by appropriately rooting them to their generational past. In so doing, we secure our own place in the cycle of generations.

Tears welled when the music teacher exclaimed, "Oh my goodness, he has perfect rhythm." My heart soared with the feeling that my musician father was there in little Harrison.

My personal experience spans five generations. First is my grandparents' generation, all born in the 1880s, who immigrated from Eastern Europe to America seeking freedom; then come my parents, born at the turn of the 20th century, who were challenged to assimilate and "make it" in this new land; next is my own generation, the children of the '30s depression era; there followed the birth of my children in the '50s and '60s, the anti-establishment flower children; and now, in the present, are my grandchildren of the '80s and '90s, the computer age. As we face the new millennium, I have a personal sense of more than one hundred years of history, from the time of the first electric light to the information superhighway. This historical perspective provides a broad view of life. It is the basis of grandparental wisdom. We have unique lessons to teach: patience, tolerance for change, security in the knowledge that one prevails in spite of the vicissitudes of life. Contemplating the span of our lives is an opportunity for reconciling our place in history.

As a judge in Family Court I knew that finding a caring adult to connect to a kid in trouble gave him a chance to succeed. When I could find such a person, often a grandparent, it made the difference.
ART O'DEA

After doggedly sticking it out in a cake-walk contest, five-year-old Caitie was victorious. "See that girl over there," she said, pointing to a classmate. "She told me I'd never win." Then Caitie turned to me and said, "Grandma, I'll never give up." I recognized her determination, a family trait. I was assured, she's one of us.

What My Grandparents Meant to Me

Grandparents and grandchildren have a lot in common.
They have a common enemy.
SAM LEVINSON

Who is their common enemy? Why the authorities, of course, the ones in charge, our children, our grandchildren's parents.

Grandchildren and grandparents can fulfill a powerful need in each other to be listened to, to have one's thoughts and ideas taken seriously, and to be cherished with few if any demands placed upon each other, except to be.
DR. MARY CERNEY

That we are both at the parents' mercy is our common bond. Our position does have particular advantages, however. Grandparenthood has distance built into it. We enjoy freedom from the requirement of daily correcting and disciplining. Unlike the parents, we are not overwhelmed by the daily care of children, nor must we subordinate our outside interests to childrearing. Besides, our experience as parents gives us perspective beyond the moment. We are less upset by the grandchildren's problems. Our acceptance of them is unburdened by criticism.

A story told by Victor Hugo about his granddaughter exemplifies the camaraderie and empathy that develops between grandparents and their grandchildren:

"My granddaughter was made to sit in a closet with no food as a punishment. When I snuck her a cookie, I said, 'I could get in a lot of trouble for doing this. They may put me in the closet.' She answered, 'Don't worry Grandfather, then I will bring you a cookie.'"

Fred Rogers, of the children's television program *Mr. Rogers' Neighborhood,* tells a story of his maternal grandfather, nicknamed "Ding-Dong" after the day he taught him the nursery rhyme, "Ding, Dong, Bell," that is illustrative of how grandparents and grandchildren become allies.

> As a youngster, I loved Sunday afternoons at Ding-Dong's farm. I was a city boy and used to a fairly formal life, which meant keeping things neat and in place. The farm had old stone walls running around it, and I wanted more than anything to be allowed to climb them and walk along their winding tops. When I was eight, Ding-Dong let me do it—over the protests of my parents. "If the boy wants to climb the stone walls," he said to my mother and father, "then let him climb the stone walls. He has to learn to do things for himself." I had the time of my life. My delight was obvious, and Ding-Dong shared it.
>
> When Ding-Dong overrode my parents' objections and gave me permission to walk on his stone walls, he didn't undermine their authority. Life at home went on as it always had. My parents were still my parents. What he did was let me know that it was possible to have different kinds of loving relationships with different people, and that I had a special place in this world as a grandson, in addition to a special place as a son.
>
> At the end of the day he gave me the message that I pass on to my television friends each time I make a new program. "Fred," he said, "you made this day a special day by being yourself. Always remember there's just one person in this world like you . . . and I like you just the way you are."

I wonder how many grandparents realize how deeply confirming their presence can be to a young child. In a relationship with a grandparent, a child can be freed of a lot of the daily expectations that are part of home life and are necessary for growth at home. A grandparent is a very special kind of ally in a child's search for an identity that includes being lovable and loving.

Many of my patients have expressed an abiding love for their grandparents and a longing, far into adulthood, for the unconditional love and comfort they once received from them. As I have listened over the years, I've found that a great deal of the happy memories of childhood have to do with grandparents. The lasting value of a grandparent's contribution is powerfully evident in these individual stories. They are empowering.

I've interviewed hundreds of people and am excited by the enormous outpouring of love and gratitude so many have expressed for grandparents. Their stories are a testament to the numerous ways grandparents make a difference. A common theme for many grandchildren is, "I would never have made it without my grandparents." These declarations clearly tell of the new possibilities we offer. A grandparent's influence is beyond measure. These stories are instructive as examples of how it's done.

"I want my Grandma," sobbed my patient, an attractive, stylish professional woman in her early forties. Although she generally functioned well, at this moment life was challenging her. She was tired and longed for the comfort she had found as a child only with her grandparents.

"I went to stay with my grandparents every other weekend while I was growing up," she told me.

"What is it that you want?" I queried.

"Acceptance. Being loved. My Grandma loved me for me. I could just be. She didn't find fault with me. If I wanted a chocolate shake at eight o'clock at night, she'd make it. When I got older, I could even have boys walk me from school to her house. My parents didn't approve of my talking to boys who were not in our church. At Grandma's and Grandpa's, life was different. I felt okay. There were no demands for me to be different, and I wasn't judged."

The acceptance and pleasure this woman received from her grandparents and the relief of living without rigid demands has been woven into her adult life.

"I would never have made it without my grandparents," a thirty-something survivor of an alcoholic mother and divorce said wistfully to me. "I went to my grandparents' farm in Tennessee every summer. It was a haven. I received unconditional love. It's wonderful to be accepted for myself. I was taken care of with the warmth my own mother couldn't give me. In fact, at home I was more of a mother to my own mother, who was usually in bed drunk. Things seemed normal when I was with my grandparents, like I was part of a family. I had fun with my cousins, and I loved the animals and the out-of-doors."

This patient's unmet needs resulted from the role reversal of having to be mother to her own mother and from having been abandoned by her father. Her only contact with normal family interaction and its warmth and fun and with the possibility of having her own needs attended to occurred during summers with her grandparents. There her needs were met, and she experienced possibilities she otherwise would never have known. There she was given hope, which continues in her life today.

A young man who has succeeded in spite of abusive parents describes how he developed self-esteem. "I didn't get admiration or encouragement from my parents, but my grandma said, 'You can do anything, Jimmy.' It was unconditional love with no expectations. I didn't have to earn it."

Another example from a forty-three-year-old professional woman and mother of two sons describes how her grandparents saved her from her mother's rejection. "When I was a child, my mother actually admitted she didn't like me. My grandparents saved my life. I really felt loved by them, and I didn't get that at home. I still carry their pictures in my wallet. Although they're no longer alive, my connection to them remains. Grandmother cut out pictures from magazines and made scrapbooks for me. They helped me to know that what was inside me as a dream was real."

"When I was eighteen, I was really wild," said Anne, a twenty-three-year-old manicurist. "My mother was too close to me. She would get upset, angry, scared. I moved in with my grandmother. My grandmother would just listen and give me room to make my own decisions. We had a ball. Grandparents are neat! I had room to find myself. They didn't pressure me with, 'What are you going to do?' I decided on my own. One day while sitting on the couch I said, 'I think I want to be a manicurist.' Grandma said, 'Okay,' and the next day she took me to a beauty school, and it all worked out."

Baby Dee, if you can think it, you can do it.
Grandfather's words that made the difference for Dionne Warwick

This is a good example of how the emotional distance of grandparenthood allows us to be more accepting of behavior that parents can't tolerate. This is particularly useful during adolescence and young adulthood, when parents are worrying and suffering over the risks children take and the uncertainty of their future.

An attractive seventy-year-old grandmother still remembers her grandmother's influence. "I was a very plain little girl. No one paid much attention to me. My mother spent hours fussing over my sister's long curls while telling me I was the *tailored type* and sending me to the barber for a short bob. I knew, though, that I was my grandmother's favorite. Everyone should be someone's favorite. She made me feel special, and that gave me hope.

"I have many positive memories. She told me Bible stories and studied the Torah. She was a fantastic cook. Thanksgiving dinners

Tell me and I'll forget. Show me, and I may not remember. Involve me, and I'll understand.
NATIVE AMERICAN SAYING

were fabulous. I never asked enough questions. My own children had no grandparents. It is a gap in their lives. That's why my husband and I want to be terrific grandparents."

"I remember my grandmother well, especially the rhythms of her language." Athlete Kareem Abdul-Jabbar spoke of his Trinidad-born grandmother.

"The traditions of folklore and storytelling are strong in the West Indies, and in her musical patois my grandmother used to tell me vivid stories about vampires and other zombie stuff straight out of West Africa.

"Her stories taught me that behind me was something real and authentic and dignified, and this helped give me some self-worth as a child. I always had the feeling of pride in where I came from. This probably saved me, especially in the neighborhood, and no doubt buoyed me during wrenching times like the civil rights struggles in the 1960s. We are not ashamed of ourselves. We go all the way back to the great black kings of West Africa. That's in me."

Making a Plan

Life is what happens while you're making plans.

All that we know from personal experience calls us to dispel the myth that grandparenting just comes naturally, that we can just sit back and enjoy. It's more complicated than that. Our children certainly didn't come with instruction books, and neither do grandchildren. Our love and good intentions are not enough. That is why we need a plan.

You can be anything you set out to be, but first you must set out.

MARGARET MEAD

We know that planning brings order to our thoughts. A plan will guide our natural emotions and intensify the pleasures of relationship. By making a plan we make conscious those feelings that do come naturally, the love we want to give, the anxiety over how to show it, and the limits for sharing it. We acknowledge what is natural and face the questions posed by our real intentions.

Thinking about our role and what we want to do introduces this key ingredient of intentionality. Intentional actions are planned with an anticipated outcome. By providing purpose for our actions we connect to their deeper meaning and derive the inner satisfaction that comes from meeting goals. Having a plan charts our course and provides a framework for action.

This grandparenting planning guide consists of four steps:

In the Lakota Sioux Nation the grandfather creates the first bow and arrow for his young grandson and uses it to teach the youth the customs and responsibilities that men have to their people. Likewise, the grandmother creates a doll for her granddaughter that is used to explain the tribe's heritage and the granddaughter's future responsibilities. These gifts, obvious signs of love from grandparents, are special gifts cherished for life.

1. Discovering your grandparenting intentions
2. Deciding what to do: making your intentions reality
3. Determining how to do it: implementation
4. Evaluating

By following these steps you will develop a blueprint for grandparenting. While anticipating that time and experience will reshape your plans, your guide will help to realize your ideal.

STEP 1. Discovering Your Grandparenting Intentions

Begin by developing your grandparent ideal with an awareness of your wishes and dreams. Organize your intentions by posing these questions:

What kind of grandparent do I want to be? _____
_____

What grandparenting models can I look to? _____
_____

How do I imagine my role? _____
_____

What kind of relationship do I want to have with my grandchildren?
_____
_____

What heritage of family values and traditions do I want to pass on?_____

A person can't go after what
he doesn't know.

_____

What are the family's needs? _____
_____

What kind of difference do I want to make?

_____

_____

_____

_____

What are my special or unique resources?

_____

_____

_____

I'm an artist and I love to teach my grandchildren. I encourage them to paint what they feel, not what they see. It's fascinating to see them get in touch with their feelings and reveal them. It leads to wonderful talks about what really matters to them. It creates a real bonding.

How much time can I give? How much time do I want to spend?

_____

_____

STEP 2. Deciding What to Do: Making Your Intentions a Reality

The second step guides you to discover how to make your ideal a reality. It requires identifying the actions and activities that will carry out your intentions. For example, how do you show your grandchild your love? First of all you must show up or be in evidence; that is 90 percent of success. After that there are infinite possibilities. Choose what seems appropriate for the moment and keep developing more ideas for later. Ideas may be as simple as making a phone call or sending a postcard or a little surprise. Others are more time consuming, like getting together to play, read or talk things over. Still others require more planning, like knitting a sweater, making a toy, working on a project together or going on an outing. More elaborate plans may include having a family dinner or holiday celebrations and visits.

It was not uncommon for the busy creative genius Alexander Graham Bell to take time from his work in his laboratory to welcome a grandchild's visit and to help with homework. In his lab, Bell encouraged his grandchildren to try simple experiments. Then he created a collection of experiments appropriate for young people.

What kinds of things do I enjoy doing? _____

_____

Plan activities that you enjoy and avoid those that you don't like. For example, if you recoil at amusement parks, as I do, then don't plan an outing to one. Doing what is pleasurable to you ensures a better outing.

What gives me the greatest pleasure when I'm with my grandchild? _____

_____

_____

What are my special skills?_____

_____

_____

_____

What stories can I tell about myself, their parents' childhood or the family? _____

_____

How can I pass on family traditions and establish new ones?

_____

_____

How can I arrange to give the most precious gift of my time?

_____

_____

STEP 3. Determining How to Do It: Implementation

This step requires translating your ideas into action. You'll need to set priorities as you allocate your time and resources. Implementation may require research. For example, if you want to instill your love of music in your grandchild, you'll need to find musical programs, tapes or instruments or, perhaps, radio or television programs you can share even when you're not together.

How will I coordinate my time with the grandchild's availability?
_____

_____

What community resources provide opportunities for experiences?
_____

_____

How can I help in their growth and development? _____
_____

What toys and books will benefit their development? _____
_____

_____

What can I do to share my interests? _____
_____

What new experiences can I introduce? _____
_____

What can we do to just be together? What can we do to have fun?
_____

_____

STEP 4. Evaluating

The fourth step is an evaluation. How did it go? Did it have the desired effect for you? . . . for the grandchild? . . . for the family? Feedback offers an opportunity to savor experience and make improvements. It's the way we learn.

What did I like about this experience? What might I change to make it more satisfying for me? _____
_____

How can I measure the response of the grandchildren and their parents? Have I asked for their input? _____

_____

_____

Was the project or outing or book age-appropriate? _____

_____

It is far more clear to me now that a society that has ceased to care about children, a society that cuts off older people from meaningful contact with children, a society that segregates any groups of men and women in such a way that they are prevented from having or caring for children, is greatly endangered.

MARGARET MEAD

Did I get the child's attention? _____

_____

_____

_____

_____

What did I learn about my grandchild that will guide my future plans? _____

_____

_____

What new ideas did I get from this experience? _____

_____

_____

_____

Let your answers serve as a guide and inspire your creativity. We can learn from the Japanese concept of *kaizen,* which means progress, by constant and steady, small improvements. It's a reminder that progress is made of many small steps, that the element of time, of pace, of appropriate moment must monitor our actions.

A journey of one thousand miles begins with a single step.
LAO-TZU

As you read this book and chart your grandparenting path, ask, "What small step can I take today? Does it follow the path which I have developed in my plan?" The true joy of grandparenting is in the journey itself, in the unity of dreaming and doing. That process enriches our lives.

Dreams are often thwarted by the lack of operational planning and impatience with small steps. We can help our grandchildren realize their dreams by teaching this concept with the example of world-class athletes and musicians who pursue their goals with patience, step-by-step, measuring each incremental improvement. That is *kaizen* at work.

By its nature, planning proceeds from the broad and the general to the narrow and the particular, from goals to objectives to process. Process involves strategy, priority, timing, resources, execution and evaluation. Your values are at work in each stage of planning, as a constant measure.

This method of intentional planning gets easier with use and will become second nature.

Isn't There Always Something?

Planning doesn't mean that grandparenting becomes worry-free, that everything goes smoothly. In fact, as grandparents, we find ourselves with all kinds of new worries, some minor and some major. We worry about how the kids let the baby cry, or how to tell our daughter-in-law that she should call the doctor about the baby's fever, or that there's too much

I wish they'd get settled once and for all so I wouldn't have to worry. Just when I thought my son and daughter-in-law were set with good jobs and a nice neighborhood with lots of kids, they may lose their jobs and are contemplating an out-of-state move.
GRANDPA SID

TV, or how to say no when asked to babysit without feeling guilty. We worry about our children's marriages working out and about their health and finances. Yes, there's always something.

But we *do* have the advantage of hindsight and years of on-the-job training. Most things we do well don't happen accidentally. With your plan, you have taken the right step to be the best you can be, to get the most of what you want and to give the most to those who need you. You are prepared for your *essential* role: to shape the lives of your family by nurturing them. Your nurturing will have a ripple effect on the society around you.

DOs AND DON'Ts

1. DO appreciate your unique opportunities as an essential grandparent.

2. DO use your own models for grandparenting as a guide.

3. DO take time to plan your grandparenting.

4. DO give your grandparenting activities priority.

5. DON'T forget that grandparenting is good for your health.

6. DO approach your grandparenting with energy and creativity.

7. DON'T forget that your adult children need your support, too.

8. DO find ways to help your grandchildren believe in themselves.

9. DO remember, when it's rough sledding, that you may be your grandchild's main source of stability.

10. DON'T lose sight of the fact that by nurturing your family you are positively impacting your society.

3

The Tasks of Grandparenting

What Will We Pass On to Our Children?

What legacy will we leave our children? What is it that we know or do that has meaning for them? Our answers reveal the tasks of grandparenthood. As we continue to nurture and give sustenance to our family, we must take our importance in the family seriously by recognizing that we have power and must work at the tasks of grandparenting. Our world is without enough caring adults. Our children are depending on us.

This book celebrates grandparents who appreciate the fact that individuals can make a difference, those for whom qualities of heart and mind still matter. It illuminates those qualities of curiosity, joy, a willingness to take risks, a passion for excellence, the belief that one person can make the world better, the gritty determination to do it. Today those qualities, more than ever, are keys to preserving the spirit of family and the structure that holds it together.

Grandparents are the family symbol of both past and future. We provide continuity with the past, linked by experience and memory, memories of deceased family members, and the significant personal events that mark and distinguish the family history. Our existence assures them that, indeed, our family has roots, that they belong to something beyond themselves. We also foretell their future. The way we live our lives is their example of what it's like to grow old. We symbolize all this by virtue of our position, no matter what we do, but the way we choose to live our lives—our verve, our health, our parenting and grandparenting—determines whether we are positive or negative symbols. Our leadership fosters hope or despair in those close to us.

We don't have to do anything to become this family symbol; it just happens, because we belong to something larger than ourselves. To become a positive force, however, we must pay attention to the kind of life we are modeling. It requires that we cultivate our relationships and earn love and the respect that tradition accords to age and wisdom. If you've ever wished to make a difference in this world, active grandparenting provides the perfect opportunity. Not only can it change the family, it can change you as well. The interplay between generations tests old assumptions and validates or modifies family values in the context of contemporary life. The good old days, if they ever existed, are gone forever, and all family members are challenged to live in a radically changing world.

My children radicalized me in mid-life by making me live up to the values I taught them. I expect my grandchildren to do it in my old age.
SAM HURST, AGE SEVENTY-FIVE

As living examples of our beliefs and values, our families—particularly our grandchildren—are guided by our examples, by the life we model and the relationships we nurture.

Nurturing the next generation is our rightful emotional task. It keeps us emotionally healthy by demanding that we remain involved in life. It keeps us connected to youth and new ideas. It surrounds us with love and care.

The task of the elders is to teach their wisdom to the young.

This was the directive given to the bride and groom at a recent wedding, a traditional Native American Chumash joining ceremony. My husband and I were honored to participate as the symbolic elders, to hold the "wisdom sticks" for the new couple. It was a profound experience to be an elder witness in that outdoor ritual and be reminded of my place in the circle of life. I am in need of continual reminders that I am at this stage. Near the end of the ceremony the newly joined couple was given a tour of their life cycle, moving counterclockwise around the circle. As they stood before us they were looking into their future. "Now you have become elders, and your task is to teach your wisdom to the young," the Shaman instructed. We returned their "wisdom sticks" and felt the power of this symbolic transfer of gathered wisdom. We watched and listened and moved to join them as the drumming began and together we danced the circle, celebrating their future together. Their ritual tradition was preparing them for the eventuality of age, with the knowledge of their changing roles.

> *On her ninetieth birthday our grandmother continues to be a source of inspiration and strength for our family. She symbolizes our faith, values and family solidarity.*

> *Grandma held our family together. She emanated a strength, drawing on her faith. She renewed our commitment to excel and do better.*
> JOSEPH KENNEDY JR.
> on the death of his grandmother,
> Rose Kennedy, at 104

Grandparents have a unique contribution to make to their grandchildren and families. Consider these our greatest offerings:

1. Unconditional love and acceptance
2. Modeling a good life
3. Providing family continuity
4. Ensuring stability and security

> *Our chief want in life is somebody who will make us do what we can.*
> RALPH WALDO EMERSON

Unconditional Love and Acceptance

Everyone needs someone who believes in them, someone who accepts them without conditions. Like sale merchandise that's marked "as is," grandchildren need to be accepted with whatever imperfections they may have. It nurtures their belief that "I'm okay."

Our self-esteem and self-confidence are closely linked to the feeling of being loved and being lovable. For the most part, children look to the adults in their environment for a reflection of who they are and how they are, and grandparents provide an uncritical social mirror, overlooking flaws the best we can so whether you know it or not, your actions are teaching self-esteem, or the lack of it, all the time, developing what psychologist Rollo May called "a center of strength."

If you are having difficulty accepting a grandchild and have done the best you can, you are not alone. Acceptance is not always easy or possible. Sometimes it's just that the chemistry between you is wrong; it may be that your grandchild isn't very lovable. Such situations sometimes change over time. At the very least they require perseverance. Don't give up on your relationship too easily and, most important, be tactful so that you do no harm.

Give a little love to a child and you get a great deal back.
JOHN RUSKIN

My grandmother hurt my feelings so deeply that it's etched in my memory. When I was about thirteen or fourteen she asked me why I didn't have more boyfriends like my mother did at that age. It was an accusation I could not defend. Clearly I was deficient. I felt such shame and rage.

Love and enjoy your child for what he is . . . and forget about the qualities that he doesn't have. The child who is appreciated for what he is . . . will have a spirit that will make the best of all the capacities that he has and of all the opportunities that come his way.
DR. BENJAMIN SPOCK

Since we enjoy more freedom in our relationships with grandchildren than parents who must worry about correcting and disciplining, it's easier for us to give love with no strings attached. Erich Fromm describes parental love as unconditional " . . . yet infected by anxiety and expectations." Grandparents are free from this parental anxiety and the daily duty of discipline and expectation. Our natural alliance encourages a *we're-in-it-together* camaraderie. Our acceptance and undemanding love is, undoubtedly, our greatest gift.

The notion that it's important for children to feel good about themselves to help them realize their potential is fairly new. Past generations were wary of praising a child for fear that encouraging pride would foster conceit and a lack of humility.

Not long ago my own ninety-year-old mother told me that she owed me an apology. She was filled with remorse by her realization that she never complimented me when I was growing up for fear that it would "go to my head." She continued by trying to make up for it. Her compliments and support felt wonderful to me, even now, as a mature professional woman and grandmother, proving you're never too old. This incident caused me to revisit my own childhood, remembering the power of my longing for my mother's approval.

Today we have a better understanding of the importance of the *I-can-do-it* feeling called self-esteem. We know that pride, self-respect and just plain liking ourselves affects our behavior and the way we see the world. The state of California recognized this with the establishment of the State Commission on Self-Esteem to study its genesis and to create strategies and programs for developing these good feelings in our children. But first of all, these good feelings must emanate from the family.

Our self-esteem is related to how we think others perceive us. When we receive positive words about ourselves it reinforces our good feelings. Negative words and punishments reinforce negative feelings and promote self-doubt. This is an ongoing and ever-changing process. No one just finally feels good about herself or himself once and for all. Self-worth is tied to our success in life's experiences by the loving and caring words and actions of those around us. Our sense of identity is fluid and mutable. Vicki Lansky's metaphor expresses it well:

Self-esteem is not a safe-deposit box, filled at one point in our life, locked, and there forever. Rather it is like a bucket of water with a hole in it (and some of us have larger holes in our bucket than others) that must continuously be refilled to stay at a healthy level when it's been leaking for a while.

A grandparent's unconditional love can refill that bucket and, I suspect, even make those holes smaller. We can assure our grandchildren that they are special and help them gain confidence to try new things and meet life's challenges with assurance. Of course, this only works when our sentiments are sincere.

Don't be complacent, feeling that they know how crazy you are about them because you've already told them how special they are. You are never finished. There is an apocryphal story told about the great English actor Sir Laurence Olivier that clearly illustrates the human need for reminders of our self-worth.

Upon meeting the great bard backstage after a performance a fan exclaimed, "Oh, Sir Laurence, I don't have to tell you what a superb performance you gave. I don't have to tell you what a great actor you are. I don't have to tell you how much pleasure you have given me." To which Olivier responded, "Oh, but you do, you do."

Loving our grandchildren is usually not difficult, but we must do more than feel it. We've got to show it, too. Feeling love in our heart for a child is not enough. We need to express our love through words and actions, being ever mindful of what we say and do, because it matters. It requires setting our priorities and deciding what counts. When grandchildren are grown and have children of their own, none of us will remember if our beds were made or the house was tidy or what the kids' grades were, but we'll all remember the quality of our relationships—the talks, outings

I recognize that unless we start early, unless we intervene early, unless we give a child a childhood that could build a firm foundation, we could never build enough juvenile justice institutions or enough prisons to deal with that child.
ATTORNEY GENERAL
JANET RENO, UCLA
commencement address 1995

and laughs. Those are the building blocks of a loving, lasting friendship with grandchildren that enables them to soar as individuals. Isn't that the goal?

Because all grandchildren need to know that they are loved and important and that they belong to a family, I have included some useful phrases for communicating that you are aware of them and recognize who they are and what they do. As you read them, think about how to personalize them and of the actions that might accompany the words.

I like you just the way you are.
Watching you grow makes me happy.
I'm glad you were born a boy/girl.
You are a part of me, an important part.
Because of you, I will live beyond my time.
I enjoy doing things for you.
I love spending time with you.
Nothing you do will ever make me stop loving you.
You can be proud of your heritage; I will tell you about it.
Take time to grow up; there is no hurry.
I'm interested in the things you do.
I want to know what you think.
I care about how you feel.
Your fears are not silly.
I will always take time to listen to you.
I will listen without judging or criticizing you.
I want to be a part of your life.
You can depend on me to protect you.
I'm proud to be your grandparent.
Don't be afraid to try new things and take risks.
I'm a safe person for you; you can tell me your problems.
I have room in my heart to love many people.
You don't have to do anything to earn my love.
I want you to know who I am as a person.
I want to have a relationship with you.
I would like to teach you what I know.
I want you to have a good life.
Feel free to ask me for what you want.

I've learned from my mistakes; you will, too.
Because of you I do things I haven't done in years.
I think about you often.
I don't want to disappoint you.
I learn from you.
Children don't cause divorces; parents do.
You help me remember my own childhood.
You help me remember when your mom/dad was little.
Because of you I see the wonder of the world.
You've given my life new purpose.
I have fun thinking about things you might like.
Teach me how to be the best possible grandparent.
You are always in my heart.
Let's have some fun together.

(adapted from *Words Every Child Must Hear*
Cynthia Good)

Your comforting words help your grandchildren overcome their fears and feel safe. Your encouraging words teach them about their own strength and your belief in them. Communicating your love and connection teaches about relationship and unconditional love. Verbalizing your own thoughts and feelings deepens your relationship. Through your words and actions they come to know you and your philosophy of life.

The Favorite

Inside each of us is a longing to be the only one, the favorite. Sharing, especially when it comes to love and attention, is not easy. That's what sibling rivalry is about. Grandparents can make the dream of being a favorite come true for their grandchildren by devoting undivided time to each. Make sure to plan time to focus on one alone. It is very powerful for both of you. Remember that this circumstance of being the one-and-only is not only rare but, even when it does occur, unsustainable. However, that doesn't invalidate those marvelous moments when longing and reality coincide. In fact, it makes them more precious.

Grandpa Art told me about his dedication to his youngest grandson, Patrick, who is clearly the underdog to his athletic brother in their father's eyes. Father is a macho kind of guy who is impatient with Patrick's more sensitive nature. So Grandpa makes it a point to draw Patrick out at the dinner table, to plan activities with him, and to find ways that show him he's special. Recognizing the difference he has set out to make in Patrick's life, Grandpa Art takes his grandparenting seriously. "When I'm not grandparenting enough, I feel dissatisfied with myself. Sometimes when I'm on the golf course I think to myself, Why are you out here? You need to be with a grandchild. That's what is really important."

Grandma Ann was almost giddy as she threw her arms around me in gratitude. She was so relieved to hear me speak of my special connection to my first-born grandchild, Caitie. "I love them all," I told her, "but Caitie and I have a special relationship. We're soul mates." "Oh, thank you," she practically squealed with delight. "Thank you for giving me permission to have a favorite." Then she explained that because of his close proximity she spent much more time with Peter, the youngest of her three grandchildren, and felt more connected to him. He was her favorite, but obviously she was troubled by her secret. It's very common to have a stronger connection to one of your grandkids. In fact, it's quite normal and doesn't mean you don't love the others, too. This is not a Sophie's Choice. It doesn't mean your relationship with the others can't be significant. Sometimes that special bond is with the first born, the one who made you a grandparent in the first place, or the first of your own gender, or the one who's most like your family, or the one who lives nearby, or like Grandpa Art's grandson Patrick, the one who you feel needs you the most. There's a certain chemistry at work that's not in your control. Seeing Grandma Ann's relief is a reminder of how important it is to accept your feelings as human and without judgment so they don't create guilt and interfere with relationships. If you do have a favorite grandchild, it is not a betrayal of the others. You can still love and appreciate them. You are still essential to their lives.

Sometimes a grandparent has admitted to me that they find a particular grandchild unlikable. It is worth trying to identify what it is about that child that you find intolerable. Does this child remind you of someone you don't like or have a trait you abhor in yourself? Does she have a special problem or seem aloof and rejecting of you? Recognizing and accepting these feelings is the most important step to becoming comfortable with the situation and discovering ways you might connect. Remember that children go through stages that may cause them to behave in ways you don't like. Perhaps it's at these times that they need our understanding the most.

Modeling a Good Life

Your way of life sets a standard for your children and grandchildren. It's your responsibility to lead the family. The way you live your life—your values, attitudes and actions—sends a loud and clear message to those who follow you. When you live your life with energy and purpose, you signal hope for the future. You send the message that it's a good life and that it continues to be worthwhile as one gets older. On the other hand, an unfulfilling life is discouraging to those who look to you to see what the future holds. For these reasons, it is important to your family that you like your life, that you have come to some resolve and acceptance that it is the life you were meant to lead. Rather than looking to the past with regret, it is healthier to learn to look forward to the things you have yet to do.

"Do as I say, not as I do," doesn't wash.

Academy Award winning actor Liam Neeson may be a hot property in Hollywood, but he hasn't forgotten the fundamentals he learned from his family growing up in Northern

Ireland, like accepting responsibility and keeping your word. His role as Oskar Schindler in *Schindler's List* and approaching fatherhood got him to thinking about fundamental principles: courage, honor, responsibility, love.

"My family were humble, hardworking people. There's a lesson in that. I learned the fundamentals of what's important, such as getting food on the table and keeping a roof over our heads and clothes on our backs. There was no selfishness. I was an altar boy, but we weren't 100 percent religiously oriented. No sackcloth and ashes. Just a lot of emphasis on education."

Liam Neeson showed he hadn't forgotten those values when he won an Oscar nomination for his depiction of Oskar Schindler. Suddenly the forty-two-year-old actor was flooded with scripts. For the first time in his twenty-year career, he was receiving star treatment—and he rejected it. He left Hollywood and, for a year, made no movies.

GAIL BUCHALTER

Expand your horizons. Get involved in something outside yourself. The mind is a muscle that requires exercise just as your body does. Keep it working. Also, devote time to keeping physically fit. Poor health interferes with the best of intentions. Participate in activities that relieve stress. Find the right diet. Every healthy thing you do for yourself makes you a more positive model for your family. The personal becomes a family matter.

Our grandparents didn't just attend church. They lived the Christian lifestyle as well. That inspired us children to do the same.

LOS ANGELES TIMES

Shortly after my father's death, my mother announced, "I have a new job." Certainly, her recent job had been caring for Dad. That announcement and the enthusiasm that accompanied it lifted the spirits of the whole family. First of all, she was signaling that there was life after loss, even as profound a loss as losing her lifelong partner. At eighty-two years old, she was tackling a brand new project and trying herself out in a brand new way. Her new job, teaching acting at the Braille Institute, gave her life a new focus as she searched the libraries and bookshops for appropriate scenes from plays to use in class. She met new people and learned new skills that built on her past career as an actress. Her ability to embrace life in the face of adversity energized her family and served as an example of life's continuing possibilities for new experience. The job kept her lively by infusing her with new ideas. She was filled with new stories that made her such good company, and she was obviously feeling good about herself and her life. The children and grandchildren knew we didn't have to worry about her. In fact, she was still there for us, continuing to be our beacon of hope.

Grandma Lucy seemed resigned as she told me that her children didn't want to hear about her problems. "They don't want to hear that I'm feeling down or my arthritis has flared up. They're so involved in their own lives, evidently they just can't handle it. So I try not to mention my problems." She went on to describe her own response to her children's inability to listen to her. "I know they love me, and I don't want to add to their burdens. I enjoy my grandchildren so very much and keep my feelings to myself."

This grandmother is willing to set aside her own needs and feelings to keep peace in the family. I hope she will find a comfortable time to talk to her children about her own needs and feelings. By not doing so, she runs the risk of having her anger build to the point of explosion or turn inward and become depression. She is forgoing her right to be recognized and validated because she is unwilling to jeopardize her relationship with her grandchildren. This dignified lady is a model of accommodation as she adapts to the realistic limitations of others.

Choose to have joy and laughter. Like your life.
BARBARA BUSH,
commencement address
Wellesley College 1990

Displaying grace and equanimity under stress models a valuable lesson. The perspective we've gained over time permits us to take things in stride. When elders display the integrity to live life with zest and without fear of death, healthy children will not fear life.

When you are a member of a family, you are not just living your own life. You are influencing others in the family by your example.

Children Learn What They Live

IF CHILDREN LIVE WITH . . .

. . . criticism, they learn to condemn

. . . hostility, they learn to fight

. . . ridicule, they learn to be shy

. . . shame, they learn to feel guilty

. . . tolerance, they learn to be patient

. . . encouragement, they learn confidence

. . . praise, they learn to appreciate

. . . fairness, they learn justice

. . . security, they learn to have faith

. . . approval, they learn to like themselves

. . . acceptance and friendship, they learn to find love in the world.

DOROTHY L. NOLTE

The needs of children are widely proclaimed, and the political debate in the '90s often reminds us of the child and of the family consequence of political action, from health and welfare to crime and education. Such a time as this begs for stronger models of family continuity and stability and for grandparents who matter.

Grandchildren graze, like the deer, on the long gray hair of their grandparents that is their wisdom.

TAUTAHCHO,
Native American,
Chumash Nation

Providing Family Continuity

You are your family's connection to the past. You have much to tell. Your personal history and that of your family's is the children's link to the past. Knowing where you come from is an important ingredient in building your identity. Connecting your grandchildren to the family's roots provides that link and renews the meaning of family. Some of this may come naturally; there are many possibilities for your creative input.

We are all connected. . . .
ALBERT GORE JR.,
Democratic National
Convention, 1992

Honor your culture and religion by the way you live. Actions speak louder than words. By providing opportunities to experience your cultural heritage and your beliefs, you teach who you are. Through rituals, food, music, books and storytelling, you keep your culture alive.

Television has replaced storytelling. You can replace television with conversation and storytelling. How do you tell stories? Just tell them as they come to you. Make them up. Tell about when you or their parent was their age. There are many ways to begin and no perfect place to begin. How is it possible to bring order out of memory? Often names are the keys to remembering. Let a person who comes to mind become the starting point. By telling family stories you can create an oral tradition for your family. If you really want to get into storytelling, contact the National Storytelling Association [see Resources for Grandparents at the back of this book]. They have conferences

After my dad died, Grandma Rose showed me and Kathleen an album of old news clippings. We thought she was just sharing old memories until she showed us an ad for employment that said, "No Irish need apply." Then she admonished us to "never forget what our roots were." She was very tough and very loving.
JOSEPH KENNEDY JR.

and books of instruction and inspiration. Many of their books are collections of stories and folktales on various religious, cultural and ethnic themes that will enrich your efforts.

Writing your story is another way to leave a legacy. Grandma Betty joined a writing class at the local Adult Education and found that most of the students were there to write about their lives as a legacy for their families. "Writing your life story becomes a powerful emotional experience. The review of your own life is a meaningful act and a priceless gift."

Grandma Jule is into genealogy. Her hobby provides the family with knowledge of their history, of their time and place in the world. Her living room is filled with stacks of the papers she has gathered over years of research. It's like a library of books, letters, legal documents and photos tracing their origins from Wales and Ireland and their arrival in the New World in the 1650s.

There are many ways to provide a sense of history to your family. Choose what is compatible with your own interests. I have had my father's name and country of origin inscribed on the Wall of Remembrance on Ellis Island, where he first set foot in America from Eastern Europe. I look forward to visiting Ellis Island with my grandchildren to learn about the immigrant experience. What a great thrill it will be to help connect the children to their great-grandpa Joe. I also have a growing collection of videos, music cassettes and CDs of the films he wrote and produced or orchestrated. By sharing them with his grandchildren and great-grandchildren, they know that their great-grandpa was a man of many talents who enjoyed a multifaceted career. They are learning that his creativity is part of them, that it is in them, that they can do things, too. It is his legacy to us. Watching his films and listening to his music serve as a springboard for storytelling about him and my childhood.

Grandma Melinda is commemorating her history with a family pilgrimage. "When my mother was twelve years old she traveled with her family by covered wagon from Wheatland, Wyoming, to Kalispel, Montana. My grandmother's diary describes the trip. They nicknamed our family conestoga *Hotel de Bum* because my grandmother was always feeding the hungry strangers they found along the way." Melinda was obviously proud of both their adventurous and generous spirit. "My three children, four grandchildren and a few of my surviving cousins will rendezvous and retrace the path of that covered wagon. This time a caravan of cars will replace the covered wagons, and we'll sleep in motels. It's taken a bit of doing and will be expensive for me, since I am paying for much of it, but I know it will be worth it. It will document a part of my life story."

There is nothing higher and stronger, more wholesome and good for life than some good memory, especially a memory of childhood.
DOSTOEVSKI

A trip like this takes a good deal of advanced planning. Just getting all the family together at one time is a feat. With this trip, Grandma Melinda is linking her children and grandchildren to their past. She is giving them an opportunity to gain a rare sense of personal history, as well as that of the American West. It is a family reunion with a special agenda.

My mother's poor health and my sense of impending loss have given rise to thoughts about what I'd like to know before it's too late. I realized that I didn't have the recipes for many of her special dishes and meals she loved to prepare. She was a great cook, and when she knew we were coming, her first question was always, "What would you like me to make for you?" I began a series of tape-recorded interviews. Then, reaching into my childhood, I added some of my favorite foods and those of my brother's and family stories they brought to mind and turned them all into a book that I typed on my computer. By the way, some of the recipes were quite simple, just homey, everyday fare like my favorite childhood dessert of chocolate pudding. Although it was made from a mix, Mother served it in lovely stemmed glasses that enhanced the experience with an air of elegance. I remember that special sense of anticipation whenever I discovered them waiting in the refrigerator for our evening meal.

Mother's ninetieth birthday provided the perfect occasion for the presentation. The book is loosely bound so that pages can be added. A glamorous photo from her early acting days shows through the clear plastic cover, with the title, *Redhair's Recipes*. It's a beautiful future heirloom that was easily and inexpensively created at my local copy mart. Mother was thrilled, and so were the family members, who were each given one. Their response encouraged me to expand the book to include a favorite recipe and photo from each of them. Suddenly, what began as a personal response to my mother's failing health grew into a family record including some lifelong family friends. I've

Seven-year-old Caitie entered the horse show arena, watched by an entourage of supporters. In the audience were a step-grandmother, a grandfather and step-grandfather, two aunts and uncles, two cousins, her parents and sister. How could she help but win?

sent copies of *Redhair's Recipes* to members of the family who couldn't attend the party, asking them for their recipes. This addition has brought much joy to those who examine the family archives. I can't describe the deep satisfaction I feel to have provided a link in the chain.

Family gatherings and reunions nourish us by giving form to what we know is important. We seek connections and need to develop a sense of belonging in order to reduce our inevitable aloneness that is an unavoidable part of the human condition. The family circle, no matter how flawed, embraces us.

Foods provide familiar tastes and smells that become experiences in themselves, celebrate our heritage, and are symbols of family, cultural and religious traditions; they provide lasting memories. The act of eating together is a ritual that creates a sense of community. In the family it is a ritual under assault, difficult to honor in the overworked, latchkey way of life of so many contemporary families. We can recognize and regret the "Fast-Food Family" and the "TV Dinner Family" while we struggle to preserve the "Sit-Down-to-Dinner Family" that we knew as children.

We are not here alone nor for ourselves alone, but we are an integral part of higher, mysterious entities against whom it is not advisable to blaspheme.
VACLAV HAVEL
Harvard commencement address

Not only do work habits, time, and the stress of economic necessity shape such family habits, there is also a failure to recognize and value the shared time in intimate conversation around the family table. We make an invaluable contribution to our children by recreating the lost experience of the family meal.

There are so many ways to provide family continuity, many quite simple and self-evident: by observing cultural and religious rituals; through photos, books, films, recipes, letters, diaries and music; by the respect shown to the preservation of memorabilia like Grandma's tablecloth, Grandpa's violin or the steel combat helmet he wore in the jungles of Guadalcanal. There is a place and a need for honest tradition and genuine nostalgia, lest we give over to movies, television and the fantasy of virtual reality

Home is the place where, when you have to go there, they have to let you in.
ROBERT FROST

the task of bringing forward the images of our past. The transient nature of modern life, along with the dislocation and dissolution of families, brings us now to think about stability and security.

Ensuring Stability and Security

Stability: the quality of being firmly established; enduring; lasting; unlikely to fall or be overthrown; likely to remain erect and retain value.

Security: the condition of being protected; safe; confident; assured; free of doubt, care, anxiety and apprehension.

Understanding these meanings allows us to look at metaphors for stability and security and the ways in which grandparents might contribute to keeping their family on an even keel with the calm resolve to endure.

Earth is bountiful, and we were surrounded with the blessings of the great mysteries.
CHIEF LUTHER STANDING BEAR, Oglala Sioux

Our literature is full of the symbols of stability drawn from nature: the earth, the mountains, the rock, the tree, the garden.

The biblical account of creation places man in the garden, alone, faced with his aloneness, his dependency, his need to make choices, and, ultimately, his guilt over "eating of the fruit of good and evil." Thus this ancient story sets the stage for the intimate union which is family. The history of the family confirms the dependence of family members upon each other and the impact of environment and place in assuring the survival, increase and well-being of our species.

Family has the greatest bearing on our country. The major cause of problems in the cities is the dissolution of families. We must ease the burden of raising a child.
GEORGE BUSH

The *structural stability* of the family speaks of order, size and configuration of habitat—which is home and place, parents, grandparents, aunts and uncles, perhaps cousins by the dozens.

The *economic stability* of family demands a steady flow of the basic material necessities for health and well-being—at least a minimum of air, water, food, clothing and shelter.

The *emotional stability* of family calls for and depends upon love, identity, confirmation, fidelity, tolerance and understanding, truly the ground of solidarity and personal and family security.

In her powerful inaugural poem, Maya Angelou evokes the image of rock and river in celebration of the stability of our American political system and in our churches the faithful sing "Rock of Ages, cleft for me, let me hide myself in thee." How difficult to find those safe places to build secure relationships in family life. How essential the role of grandparents.

Grandparents are called to participate in creating family stability in all its dimensions. First, you must show up, you must be available, you must spend time. Remind your family that you are there, that you think of them, that you represent a place, a rock, an anchor in the turbulent sea of change. Assure them that their lives are entwined with your own, that you will not drop out and not be missed. Persuade them that the time is *now* to deepen and extend vital family relationships.

In a little book of sermons, theologian Paul Tillich examined *The Eternal Now.* "We go towards something that *is not yet,* and we come from something that *is no more.* We are what we are by what we came from. It is hard for us to imagine *being-no-more.* It is equally difficult to imagine our *being-not-yet.* We think: *now* we are; this is *our* time . . . and we do not want to lose it."

Can we understand that we—grandchild, parent and grandparent—live together in this eternal now? We can make it something special before some of us face the *being-no-more.* That is also Tautahcho's message: "Some have just come from the spirit world and some are on their way there." As Erich Fromm posits, "Our lives are framed by the conflict between routine and the attempt to get back to the fundamental realities of existence. We can fulfill ourselves only if we remain in touch with these fundamental facts, if we can experience the exaltation of love and solidarity, as well as the tragic fact of our aloneness and of the fragmentary character of our existence." Getting in touch with these ultimate realities of life is possible through our natural task of grandparenting. It is a significant way of breaking through the surface of routine and plumbing the depths of meaning.

Grandparents provide a safety net for stability and security, for us to know that we are not alone. We are not so sufficient unto ourselves that we can exist easily without connection and family support. We all have moments of profound inadequacy, when we need each other. By lending an ear to your children and grandchildren, sharing your thoughts and giving encouragement during times of doubt, you calm fears and reduce their sense of isolation. Your efforts to meet their needs give them strength, not just to endure but to prosper. You also make it easier for them, in turn, to give you encouragement and support. Relationships are, after all, a two-way street.

The accepting nature of our relationships with grandchildren makes it easier for them to be open and to confide in us. Our vantage point, our third perspective, makes our responses potent. *When grandparents talk, grandchildren listen.*

We provide a safe haven in the midst of social turbulence. Children are losing their childhood too soon. We need to help them stay children as long as possible. Not only are they entitled to that, we owe it to them because it promotes healthy development. There is a prevailing assumption that young children are competent and don't require authority, that they can handle the kind of autonomy and decision making that is appropriate to adults. In addition, the line between adolescence and adulthood is being erased. Our grandchildren need the comfort and protection of rules and structure, but instead, they are abandoned to a hypnotic trance in front of the TV. They need space to experiment and play, safe neighborhoods and schools. They need the nurturance and protection that provides an umbrella of security and stability.

Maggie Kuhn, founder of the Gray Panthers, once wrote that she would like her gravestone inscribed: "Here lies Maggie Kuhn under the only stone she left unturned."

When I asked Grandma Maxine about her two weeks of babysitting her grandsons, ages seven and nine, tears came to her eyes. She murmured, "I am so disappointed." She had great expectations when she left, plane tickets and extra spending money for special treats in hand. "They really didn't need Grandma," she continued. "I could have sent them the money I spent and let them hire a driver and a cook." A touch of bitterness crept in as she explained that the boys were so self-sufficient that they didn't relate much to her and saved all the accounts of their day for their mother's phone call at seven each evening. "I was shocked," she said, "when Larry, the youngest, told his mother that he had fallen off his bike. He hadn't said a word about it to me. I finally told them how I felt. They told their mom, and she was very upset with me. Well, if I ever do that again, I'll insist that the parents not call so often and certainly not in the evening so that the grandchildren have all night to miss them." Grandma Maxine has a point. It sounds as if the mom was controlling the household from long distance and it had the effect of shutting Grandma out. The boys were so busy living up to expectations of competence that they were unable to accept Grandma's attention.

Transience and mobility are profound disruptions to kinship ties. Although individuals count on the family as a group of people who will always be there for them, grandparents are in one spot, children in another, aunts and uncles, cousins and kissing kin elsewhere still. This makes our input to grandchildren *essential.*

Family structure is at the heart of the community. It must be maintained and strengthened through frequent contact. In a stable and settled community with the family extending several generations into the past, who you are is linked to who your family had been and what you had done as perceived by people familiar with you from childhood. In today's mobile world, this extension of the self into the past is diminished.

> "Growing up in tiny Plains, Georgia, had an impact on my life and how I feel about neighborhoods and communities and people caring about each other. As a child it was not unusual to wake up one morning and find out someone had an awful disease like pneumonia. Everybody in town would rally around. Cars would be in front of the house. Mother would cook. You'd take things in."
>
> ROSALYNN CARTER

Grandparents have a profound calling to renew the meaning of family by creating the necessary stability in all its dimensions.

> While fitting my eyeglasses, Grandpa Jerry was relating how he and his wife provided the only stability in their five-year-old grandson's life. His divorced parents are unsettled, without dependable employment, having struggled with drug addiction. They have erratic personal habits, including various sleep-over partners. "Jimmy has a real home life when he's with us. We sit down to the table together, we take care of him and let him know that he's loved. He has a chance to see what a good marriage is like."
>
> These grandparents are making a valuable contribution to their grandson who, through them, is experiencing the stable, predictable environment every child needs for healthy development.

Here's how one family ensured family solidarity when they grew frustrated watching the family grow further apart. Now, once a month, they gather at a different family member's church for Family Day. "It's an inconvenience to some family members each time, but that's what family does for each other," one of them explains. After church, they go out for lunch, then spend the rest of the day catching up. At the day's end they form a "unity chain" to pray for the protection of the family.

I can't wait to come to your ranch and take a walk and feel safe.
CELIA, 13-year-old city dweller

Stability requires the knowledge that the family is firmly established and a belief that it will endure. When, for example, a family exhibits the power of solidarity by gathering together, they are providing security for its members. Those who feel a part of a family feel protected from danger. That fosters a sense of freedom from doubt and a well-founded confidence and self-assurance. With a knowledge of home in one's person, it is possible to leave home. You can dare to go away from the safe haven of family when you know they will be there when you choose to return.

Where there is unity, there is strength.

First, you must show up; you must be available. Find ways to remind your family that you are there and that you think of them. Help them to become grounded by your values, traditions and aspirations. You are much more important than you realize. Although we seldom think about it, many people's lives are entwined with our own. We cannot drop out and not be missed.

Rituals taught me that the Rathers were a family unit, that we belonged together, that we did things together, that we were close.

DAN RATHER

THE SUNDIAL

The shadow by my finger cast,
     Divides the future from the past,
Behind its unreturning line,
     The vanished hour, no longer thine.
Before it lies the unknown hour,
     In darkness and beyond thine power,
One hour alone is in thine hands,
     The now on which the shadow stands.

WELLESLEY COLLEGE SUNDIAL

Grandma and Grandpa's house has always been in my life. It is like my compass. There is North, South, East, West, and Grandma and Grandpa's.

SUSAN, age forty

DOs AND DON'Ts

1. DO believe that you can make a difference.

2. DO be willing to take risks in your grandparenting relationship.

3. DO be willing to explore the roots of the family, even if it brings surprises.

4. DO be willing to go with the flow of change.

5. DON'T give up too quickly on a difficult relationship; work on it.

6. DO offer honest praise and sensitive criticism.

7. DO get involved in something outside yourself; keep looking for new jobs.

8. DO take time and give time.

9. DO let children be children.

4

Thinking About the Life Cycle

To everything there is a season, and a time to every purpose under the heaven; a time to be born, and a time to die; . . . a time to weep and a time to laugh; a time to mourn, and a time to dance; . . .

ECCLESIASTES 3:1–2, 4

Everyone Rides the Carousel

Do you remember how only yesterday when you were little you could hardly wait to grow up, to be bigger and older? Now here you are wondering, "Who is that older person looking back at me in the mirror?" And you're even a grandparent. How did we get here so fast? I don't feel that old. Do you?

Grandparenthood marks our passage into a new stage in the life cycle. It's a reminder of time passed and time passing. Recently, at my fortieth high school reunion, I was shocked to find that the attractive matron greeting me turned out to be the former prom queen. She certainly looked older than I felt. It was almost unbelievable to find friends from the first grade who still seemed so familiar after a lifetime. Their personalities and even their mannerisms were familiar. Why, we could have been back on the lunch benches at Rio Vista Elementary School, chatting away just as we used to do. This time, though, we weren't talking about our

Most grandparents want to enjoy a meaningful relation-ship with their grandchild. They're not sure how to do it.

school work or our Brownie meeting; we were talking about our families and our grand-children. You see, we're all grandparents now. That thought shakes me into an awareness of my participation in the inevitable cycle of life. Too soon we are part of the oldest generation in the family.

The Plan

Grandparents are usually quite clear about their desire to have a meaningful relationship with their grandchildren. They want to make a real difference in their lives but are unclear how to go about it. Understanding the plan of the life cycle provides a guide for doing it.

There is a natural plan for our personal growth and develop-ment throughout life. Physical and emotional development are not accidental. They're programmed like your computer. From beginning to end we pass through predetermined stages, each with its own meaning and purpose. For example, in the first stage of life (birth to two years), we're programmed in sequence to learn the skills needed to walk. First we sit up, then crawl, then walk. In other words we grow into a toddler and enter the next stage. Although there are individual differences in the timing, some earlier and some later, it is basically the same for everyone. So we know what to expect. It's predictable.

Emotional development in our culture has a similar plan. It's just not as easily observed. Each stage of development is orga-nized around particular emotional tasks. For example, the emo-tional tasks of the first stage revolve around the development of trust and hope. During this stage, basic attitudes about the world are being formed. The infant is answering the question, "Is this a good place to be?" Her experiences are providing the answer.

The point of view that sees the glass as half full or half empty begins here. The attitudes developed at one stage are not completely set for life. This is not an achievement scale on which we develop an attitude once and for all; it is an ongoing process, continually responsive to life experience and, therefore, changing.

The Eight Stages

The life cycle has been divided into eight stages of development by psychoanalyst Erik Erikson. These eight stages provide us with a framework for viewing life experiences and understanding the tasks that confront each stage. By studying the life cycle chart, we learn about our own passages through life and those of others. It clarifies our understanding of each family member and their needs, including our own.

Each stage has its own physical and emotional tasks. We grow in stages. Remember how reassuring it was to hear that the *terrible twos,* when your toddler was asserting herself by saying, "No," to everything, was just a stage and that she'd grow out of it? And she did.

Your toddler was in Stage Two, in which the goal is autonomy. [See chart on page 75.] She was working on becoming an independent person, separate from you. Saying, "No," loud and clear, was really an affirmation, declaring, "I am myself, not you. I am separate, with my own ideas. To prove it, when you say, 'Yes,' I will say, 'No.'" So no is really a statement of yes. "Yes, I am a person, too." Understanding this has helped many a parent avoid unnecessary confrontations with their two-year-olds. Sometimes, just smiling and taking her by the hand and leading her into the house in spite of her protest is all that's needed.

Physical development interacts with emotional development. They are interdependent. The two-year-old gains physical independence, too. The sphincter muscles develop so that she gains control of her elimination, and her new motor development provides the physical ability to be more independent. She can run away from you.

As grandparents we have the advantage of looking back and remembering what it was like for us as we traveled through life's stages, the stages our children and grandchildren are in now. The hindsight we enjoy is called wisdom. We can use it to promote better relationships with our grandchildren and children. As we think about the stages of life, we are reminded of our own stage in life and the tasks we are facing. It is crucial that we take care of ourselves and our psychological needs. If we don't, we will not only cheat ourselves of the pleasures of our age but will not function at our highest level for the family.

Actually young people are no different than their predecessors. But they operate in a different world—a world in which their elders are not certain of their own beliefs. They would be more sure of their values if we were more sure of ours.

RALPH RUTENBER, M.D.

Envisioning: A Shortcut for Understanding Others

This is an exercise to help you develop empathy, the ability to put yourself in the place of another and better comprehend them. While envisioning, you begin to understand the needs of others by recalling what you were like at their age. This will help you to get in touch with the issues that are important to them. You also relive your past, which may be painful, but envisioning gives you an opportunity to create positive outcomes for others. Here's how:

1. Set aside some time and find a quiet place for yourself.

2. Choose the person you wish to understand better.

3. Think back to the time when you were the age of that person.

4. Visualize your life then, where you lived, what you were doing, how you felt about yourself, your family and friends.

5. Remember some specific experiences and let the feelings in. Do you remember how you looked, how you dressed?

6. What did you like to do then?

7. What did you worry about?

8. What pleased you and helped you?

9. What do you wish was different about that time in your life?

10. Looking back, what do you wish you knew then?

11. After you've given yourself a good visit with the person you were at that age, think about the person you have in mind.

— What are the similarities and differences between the person and you at that age?

— What needs does that suggest?

— What are the implications for your relationship?

— What can you do?

Although many things change, many things stay the same. Our own experience offers us the understanding that helps to develop ideas for what they need, how you can connect with them and support them.

Your Tool Kit for Making a Difference

Physical development and emotional life are organized around the mastery of tasks. By establishing a person's developmental stage, you identify her emotional tasks. Keep in mind that each stage, like a building block, rests on the stability of the past. The identified task for each stage signifies the most advantageous window of opportunity for its optimum development. But emotional development is fluid and in need of continual reinforcement. For

When society sees older people as mainly a problem and not part of the solution to any of society's problems, this generates a sense of guilt and pity among the young, and not a sense of appreciation for the talents and energies that older people can still contribute to society . . . the aged come to accept this negative stereotype and act in accordance with the role of senior citizen.

VERN BENGSTON

example, trust established in the first two years must be bolstered throughout the stages and will be challenged by experience.

Another consideration to understanding development is the research of Carol Gilligan at Harvard that sheds light on the cognitive differences between boys and girls, not surprising to anyone who has raised a child. It posits that girls are socialized to be more concerned about relationships and the feelings of others and seek consensus and compromise in their decision making. Their identity is inwardly and interpersonally defined. When a female adolescent struggles to integrate her female aspiration with the more masculine competence she has acquired at school, she may fear success as loss of femininity.

Boys, on the other hand, are socialized to be more autonomous. Their decisions tend to rely on the structure of rules and authority. The active adventure that is viewed as a male activity leads them to adopt a different vision of success, one that is based on external achievement. Boys in their games are more concerned with rules, while girls are more concerned with relationships, often at the expense of the game itself. This calls us to discover ways to support positive growth and build relationships in both sexes.

It is obvious that values of women differ often from values which have been made by the other sex. Yet, it is the masculine values that prevail.
VIRGINIA WOOLF

How to Use the Chart

Here is your guide to the eight stages of the life cycle with their corresponding central tasks. Use it as you would use a road map. Locating a person's developmental stage is similar to locating a city on a map. You know just where it is, how to get there and where you can go from there. When you assist in the mastery of an age-appropriate task, take pleasure in the knowledge that you are really forging a connection to serve as the basis for a solid relationship. You will enjoy more satisfaction from your grandparenting when you are innovative. Most important, don't leave yourself out. Consider carefully the work your own stage provides for you.

To use this guide, locate your grandchild's or child's or your own stage on the chart by chronological age. Then learn about the stage, its corresponding tasks, and what you can do to promote healthy growth. Remember this is not an achievement scale. Tasks are not completed once and for all, and there are always individual differences to serve as reminders of each person's uniqueness.

THE EIGHT STAGES OF THE LIFE CYCLE

	Stage	Age	Basic Emotional Task
	1	Birth–2 years	TRUST
Your grandkids	2	2–4 years	AUTONOMY
are here	3	4–7	INITIATIVE
	4	7–13	INDUSTRY
	5	14–22	IDENTITY
Your kids are here	6	22–50	INTIMACY
You are here	7	50–65	GENERATIVITY—Nurturing the new generation
	8	65+	EGO INTEGRITY—Accepting your life with a positive attitude

Stage One: Birth to Two Years—Trust

What Is Trust?

Trust is the developing sense the infant gets about her new world. It's her answer to the question, "Is this a pretty good place to be?" If her needs are being met in a good enough fashion, the answer will be yes. If not, mistrust grows. Trust is the emotional focus of the first two years. It's formed through the experience of interactions between the inside and the outside worlds. When her inside world says, "I'm hungry," and the outside responds with food, that equals a pretty good place, a place you can trust. When the infant's needs are met—she's fed and kept comfortable and has attentive, loving care—she builds confidence that everything is okay; not to worry. The baby is calmer and more relaxed and is open to her environment.

What Is Needed to Encourage the Development of Trust?

A stable, predictable environment encourages the development of an infant's sense of trust. That translates into making certain that needs are met in a timely fashion and that the everyday world is familiar and comforting. The child needs opportunities to interact with her caretaking adults and others in her world. Keeping her world predictable means making her world dependable: the same loving people to provide care, the breast or bottle readily available, minimal frustration (it can never be fully eliminated), and stimulation that beckons the child into the outside world.

What Can Grandparents Do to Help?

1. Support your grandchildren's parents (your kids) with positive encouragement. Today's families are so stressed they need your input and support. This will give them the security and good feelings that they can pass on to their children. Find ways to help out.

Our standing gift for our children's wedding anniversary is money for a night in a hotel and our babysitting while they are gone. This way they can look forward to time together, and we get the children alone.

GRANDMA BABE

2. Babysit when you can, so that they can have some time for themselves. A good marriage provides a healthy environment for your grandchild.

3. When you greet the baby, don't startle or pounce on her. Approach gently, avoiding overstimulation, respecting the baby's own space.

4. Learn to observe the infant interacting with her world. It's not only fascinating, it will let you in on what's going on inside that little mind. For example, watching an

infant interacting with the mobile hanging over her crib, you will see the motor reflexes in action, the attempt to reach and grab, and the intensity with which the whole physical and mental being is involved. You'll get a sense of the purpose in those actions. It's wondrous.

5. Interact. Talk, sing, hug and cuddle, rock and hold her close.

6. Just love her and have fun!

Stage Two: Two to Four Years—Autonomy

What Is Autonomy?

Autonomy is another way to say, "I want to do it myself!" Your toddler is asserting herself, and her physical development is cooperating. She can walk now and even run away from you to prove she's a separate person who can do her own thing. She is learning to both hold on to you and let go, and she is getting ready to assume control of her bodily functions. The *terrible twos* are really a marvelous time of self-affirmation. It's a time when no means yes. While the toddler says, "No!" in defiance, she is actually saying, "Yes, I'm a separate person. I'm me, not you. I'm terrific." This self-will inspires acts of resistance or protested independence.

What Is Needed to Encourage Autonomy?

Avoid unnecessary power struggles. The toddler needs opportunities to try herself out in the world. She needs small victories that provide the satisfaction of "I can do it." These victories often come through opportunities to interact with her material and social environment, such as finding out how she can manipulate toys; learning to play with other children; having opportunities to be separate from the parents by going off with Grandpa; and being given time to explore with a patient grandparent, your most precious gift.

What Can Grandparents Do to Help?

1. Be patient. Don't push your toddler to hurry up and grow. Respect her own pace.

2. Be firmly reassuring when the infant or toddler is developing a new skill. Don't use shame.

3. Avoid power struggles by understanding the underlying message of defiance and self-assertion; go around it instead of meeting it head on. When the child announces, "No!" to going inside, don't argue; just smile and take her hand and take her in.

4. Keep your sense of humor.

5. Don't compare the development of one child with another. It promotes a sense of failure and jealousy. Everyone develops in her own time. What's the big deal if someone does it sooner or later? Sooner is not necessarily better or smarter.

6. Respect your children's child-rearing decisions, even if you disagree with them. Remember, it's not up to you.

7. Provide experiences that help your toddler explore her world. Take nature walks, for example, even around her own backyard.

8. Since separation from parents is a major issue (letting go), provide opportunities for your grandchild to have some positive experience with separation by going off with you.

9. Encourage social interaction with others in the family, both children and adults. This gives a toddler a sense of belonging to more than her immediate family and provides glue for family ties.

10. You need energy for this age child. Take good care of yourself. The better health you're in, the more fun!

"I noticed that my three-year-old granddaughter was rather quiet while we were driving together. I thought she should be noticing more of what was around her. As we passed a house with a bright red front door, I pointed it out to her: 'Look at that red door.' From that day on she commented on that red door every time we passed it. It worked. She began noticing more things and commenting on them. I always remember what we shared and that I made a difference."

GRANDMA REDHAIR

Stage Three: Four to Seven Years—Initiative

What Is Initiative?

Initiative provides the motivation to start an action. It is the fuel for the human motor. Because it is a prerequisite to action, it is necessary for learning and doing. Without it, we can't get started. Initiative adds to autonomy the quality of undertaking, planning and "attacking" a task for the sake of being active and on the move.

What Is Needed to Encourage Initiative?

Just when you think, *This is the best age,* it gets better. You can really hold interesting conversations. A child in this stage can help to plan projects and outings. Children this age need a lot of opportunity for planning and making and doing. They are on the go. They are ready for more separation from home and are excited by more "grown-up" experiences. They are actively learning and open to new ideas, experiences, projects. Socially they seek

When announcing the merger of his company, Turner Broadcasting, with Time-Warner for $7.5 billion, mogul Ted Turner, 56, said at the news conference, "I'm tired of being little all the time, and I'm looking forward to having muscle on our bones." How big is big? I recall an interview on national television during which Mr. Turner talked about his father's beatings when he was a boy. Obviously, the hurt and humiliation, the experience of being overpowered by a bigger person, has given him a deep sense of smallness. This becomes the driving force behind insatiable ambition in adults.

group tasks and cooperation. The dreams of early childhood become attached to the goals of adult life. This is a busy and exciting time.

What Can Grandparents Do to Help?

1. Introduce your grandchild to new ideas about the world around her.

"Grandpa needs to learn about four-year-olds."
After Grandpa carelessly caused this child to miss an important event.

2. Talk about your own response to things, your own ideas. Let them know who you are. Share your enthusiasms. Help them get turned on to life through a diversity of experiences and ideas.

3. Teach them your skills and hobbies.

4. Support new experiences and special projects.

5. They love to help and have jobs to do but will require your guidance. Some possibilities are juicing oranges, polishing silver, doing yard work, washing the car, helping with younger children. You will be able to think of other activities. Such projects make them feel good and promote a sense of responsibility.

6. Take them seriously; listen carefully and take time.

7. Never forget to bring along your sense of humor.

Stage Four: Seven to Thirteen Years—Industry

What Is Industry?

Industry sounds like work, and that's just what this new stage is about. By the time a child has reached her seventh year, she is all set for "entrance into the world." Having mastered the physical skills of movement and control over bodily functions, she has also acquired the ability to express herself with words. She is now ready to enter the world outside the family

I'm in a hurry to get things done and I don't know why. All I have to do is live and die but I'm in a hurry.

and to discover the pleasure of work. In all cultures, children at this stage receive some systematic instruction. In our culture, children must learn to be literate and receive the widest possible basic education for the greatest possible range of career choices. Yes, this is where the development of skills for future work begins.

What Is Needed to Encourage a Child's Industry?

The child at this stage needs opportunities to learn—all kinds of learning—learning new skills, learning how to make things, learning how to get along with others. A sense of inadequacy and inferiority are the dangers of this stage. The child of this age has a more complicated social reality. The school child has taken another step away from family. School is its own social world with its own demands. Socially, this is a most decisive stage.

"Mommy, why are we always in a hurry?"
This question from a five-year-old shocked her mother because it was so true. Mother had no answer.

What Can Grandparents Do to Help?

1. Do projects together, cooperatively. Since industry involves doing things with and beside others, this is the introduction to the division of labor. Bake cookies, make a birdhouse. Be creative.

2. Expand horizons. Introduce and explore just about anything—music, art, sports, nature.

3. Offer encouragement to follow their own ideas and interests, to believe in themselves. Listen, listen, listen.

4. Take outings and trips to explore the world.

5. Tell stories about when you were in school, when your kids were in school.

6. Don't be in a hurry. Children thrive on attention.

Ten-year-old Eloise is following in the footsteps of her two entrepreneur grandfathers, with their encouragement. She and her two partners, neighbors Joanna, eight, and Nathan, six, take their business seriously. They bake on Fridays (cookies, cupcakes, brownies) and sell from their stand in front of the house on Saturdays. They add vegetables harvested from their joint garden and lemonade on hot days. They are supported by regular customers and have made seventy-two dollars this summer.

Stage Five: Fourteen to Twenty-Two Years—Identity

What Is Identity?

With the advent of sexual maturity, childhood comes to an end and youth begins. The rapid body growth at this stage is similar to that of early childhood, with the added ingredient of sexual maturity. The major issues now are "Who am I?" and "What will I become?" The youth at this stage has established a good deal of competence in the world of skills and tools, but the physiological revolution within and the tangible adult tasks ahead create uncertainty. This youth stands squarely between childhood and adulthood. The danger here is confusion surrounding the questions "Who am I?" and "What will I become?" Ouch! Who doesn't remember the painful uncertainties of their own teenage years—one moment feeling strong and sure, the next absolutely dissolving in self-doubt?

What Is Needed to Foster Identity?

A sense of identity is derived from an accrued confidence in one's value to others, past and future, in the family and in work. Teenagers' appearance to others becomes crucial, because they're so unsure of their own view of themselves. That's why teenagers tend to be overly certain, clannish and sometimes cruel to others by excluding them from the group. Appearance—how one dresses or wears his hair—becomes a sign of whether he is acceptable enough to be part of the "in" group. It's important to understand (which doesn't mean to condone) such intolerance as the group members' attempt to support their own identity. They are searching for social values and ethics.

When Grandma Pauline's daughter Martha called to exclaim, "Guess what she's done now," referring to her seventeen-year-old daughter, Abby, she told of the nose-ring the girl now sported. "At least," she said in an attempt to console herself, "it's on the side of her nose and not in the middle."

Grandma asked if Abby had begun to purchase a college wardrobe for her entrance to Stanford University next month. "No, she hasn't mentioned anything about clothes," Martha answered. "Well, from what I've noticed, she doesn't seem too interested in clothes," Grandma observed. Martha began to laugh, saying, "Would you believe she spends about three hours in the morning to get that look, changing tee shirts and jeans to make sure the holes are in the right place?"

This young woman is making a statement and establishing her identity with her "look" and nose-ring. She's aligning herself with like-minded peers. I asked Grandma how she viewed her role in these issues. "I will encourage Abby to do her own thing," she declared.

This is also the age of "falling in love," which is more an attempt to find oneself than it is to find a partner. To keep themselves together, they may over-identify with heroes or groups, to the point of apparent, complete loss of identity. That's why peer pressure can be so persuasive and overrule good judgment.

Teenagers and their parents are notoriously at odds. Sometimes it's a result of a desperate attempt to become separate and find their own identity. Devaluing a parent may help the separation process; after all, if parents are so square, who needs them anyway? The more uncertain the teens are, the harder they push against their parents. Raging hormones create emotional ups and downs and moral dilemmas: peer pressure to "try it" (drugs, sex,

Your belief in your grandchild fosters her belief in herself.

driving fast), demands for freedom and independence, learning skills for careers. It's a turbulent, sometimes marvelous time. No wonder all parents of teenagers suffer.

What Can Grandparents Do to Help?

1. Be available to listen without judgment. This is not always easy, but it is important if you are going to keep communication open. Don't freak out at what you might hear; you'll lose them.

2. Keep in mind that grandchildren trust grandparents. You are in an advantageous position to gain their confidence and influence them.

3. Value them for who they are, not just for what they do.

4. Relate to them by telling them about your own experiences.

5. Talk about your philosophy of life, about what worked and what didn't.

6. Encourage them to do well in school. Explain why education is relevant to their future.

7. Support, to the best of your ability, interests you feel are positive.

8. Do everything you can to help them feel that they have a future. Having a future to look forward to provides the most compelling reason to stay in school and to say no to drugs and sex.

9. Support their parents. They need all the help they can get.

10. Have adventures together.

11. Don't bad-mouth the grandchild to the parents or the parents to the grandchild. You'll only make matters worse.

12. Keep a constructive, problem-solving approach.

13. Because teenagers are searching for social values and they love rituals, initiate or help them discover some.

Mom, you are really square, but Gram and Gramps are cool.

SUSAN, age fourteen

14. Keep your cultural heritage alive. It's an important part of their identity.

15. Provide information that promotes knowledge about and access to opportunities, e.g., jobs, schools, mentors, scholarships, activities.

16. Reach out and let them feel your support. This is the time when most grandparents become less active in their grandchildren's lives. The kids are just too busy and they may be away at school. Write, telephone, send goodies. Don't wait for them to come to you.

Grandparents know you are perfect.

ELOISE, age ten

They need you more than ever. You can be a stabilizing influence at a time when parents can't reach them.

Stage Six: Twenty-Two to Fifty Years—Intimacy

What Is Intimacy?

We now enter the stage of falling in love and then working it out. The young adult is emerging from the search for identity and is ready for intimacy, which requires a willingness to commit oneself to partnership. Intimacy means relationships, and although the needs in relationships change with age and time, they become the focus here. Just look at the newsstand or movies or TV soaps and you can see what interests most people. There is a great deal of variation in this stage, for it spans three

For a time last year I thought I might be pregnant. Not long after that I went to help my daughter with my first grandchild. It was both wonderful and exhausting. When I left I was so glad it wasn't me.

GRANDMA MARIE, age forty-eight

decades. After choosing a partner, there is the reality of working it out and then adding more relationships with children and extended families.

What Is Needed to Foster Intimacy?

The psychoanalyst Sigmund Freud was once asked what a person needs to succeed in life. He said, "To love and to work." Sounds really simple, doesn't it? Well, actually it is not as simple as it first appears. The ability to love and work rests on the foundations built in the earlier stages. In order to love well, you must be able to share mutual trust, to have a sense of identity that permits you to fuse with another without losing yourself, and to achieve intimacy in a sexual relationship. In order to enjoy work satisfaction, you must have developed the skills of past stages: autonomy, industry and identity. The danger of this stage is isolation, the avoidance of contacts that commit you to intimacy. The major focus is on loving, work, procreation and recreation.

What Can Grandparents Do to Help?

It is when our children are at this stage that most of us become grandparents. These days families need a lot of support.

1. Find creative ways to support your children's relationship and family. After all, their relationship provides the stability for your grandchild. Appreciate the challenge they face to make marriage work.

Mother is such a joy to be around; we enjoy being with her and love to take her with us when we travel.
TONI L.,
on holiday with her mother

2. Offer your wisdom gently and only when asked. *No meddling.*

3. Provide support and some relief from your children's relentless responsibilities by becoming involved with your grandchildren.

4. Become the hub for the family. Continue and create family traditions at holidays and throughout the year.

5. Be aware that you are a model for your family. That is your task. Do it well by remaining a positive and vital force. Don't become a burden.

6. Remember that you cannot look to your family to make your life. Get involved in something larger than yourself.

Stage Seven: Fifty to Sixty-Five Years—Generativity Nurturing the New Generation

What Is Generativity?

Finally, here you are! This is the time in life when most of us become grandparents. What an interesting time in our life cycle! We are young enough to savor the freedom from daily child-rearing and active enough to be pursuing our own work and interests with vigor. We can now take a moment to think about ourselves. True generativity is much more than having grand-children. It is taking an interest in guiding the next generation, our grandchildren, by getting involved with them. It means developing nurturing relationships and passing on their heritage. It focuses us on the present and the future.

In a curious way, we are dependent on our families for the focus they provide. They inform us that our lives have been extended beyond ourselves and are worthwhile. Taking stock, there is both comfort in their successes and sadness over their struggles. Accept and take pride in the family you have created. Never doubt that they con-tinue to need us. Our role with them calls into question the amount of time we wish to devote. Time is a great gift to your family and sends the loudest and clearest message of your support. The question of time extends beyond the immediate family with a mandate to embrace the needs of children everywhere. By accepting the challenge of our emotional task, we ward off the dangers of stagnation and interpersonal impoverishment.

It takes a village to raise a child.
AFRICAN PROVERB

"We live in a world where we believe nothing endures, nothing lasts. There is a crisis of meaning. Without meaning there cannot be hope. Without hope there is embitterment. We must determine what we will become. You remember Lilly, my near-perfect grandbaby? Lilly is my conscience.

When you've held that first grandbaby you know continuity in life and that you must do right now so that grandbaby will do better later."

FORMER TEXAS GOVERNOR ANN RICHARDS

How Can Grandparents Do It?

1. Nurture the family by creating good experiences. I've discovered that many of the happy memories of childhood have to do with grandparents.

2. Be a model for the possibilities of life. Don't underestimate your importance to your family.

3. Take care of your health. Nurture yourself.

4. Be productive. Do one thing each day that fosters your task of generativity.

5. Support your grandchild's parents, be accepting of their relationship and help them to have some time together.

6. Become a creative grandparent; give it time and stay involved.

7. Accentuate the positive.

8. Provide vision for your family.

9. Extend your interest in children by becoming a surrogate grandparent.

10. Be an advocate for children.

What if a person could eliminate all negative experiences in his life? Would he be free of stress?

According to researchers at the University of California at Berkeley, the answer is no. The researchers found that the presence of positive factors in life, rather than merely a lack of negative factors, was most important in reducing stress. Too much emphasis has been given to eliminating negative experiences and not enough to teaching people to develop the positive aspects of life.

THE WELLNESS LETTER
University of California at Berkeley

Stage Eight: Sixty-Five Years and More— The Age of Wisdom

What Does It Mean to Possess Wisdom?

Wisdom is not something that happens naturally as the result of age. Wisdom is the embodiment of all the eight stages. Wisdom accrues by accepting one's life as the life that had to be and is the product of resolve, resolving the issues of the past combined with tolerance toward your own parents and your choices. It combines an emotional integration of the past, a philosophical attitude toward life, and acceptance of your own mortality without despair. It also requires an acceptance of the change and loss that surrounds aging. Not an easy task.

How can we face our grandchildren if they say, "You mean, you were alive when the cheetahs were here and didn't do anything to save them?"

DAN KRAUSE,
working to save cheetahs
from extinction in Namibia

The danger at this stage is becoming a fearful, despairing person, soured on life. You are challenged to draw upon your faith, to conduct a spiritual quest that helps you maintain optimism and continue to love life. The struggles and resolutions of each conflict and task throughout the life cycle have added a richness and dimension to your understanding. It is a measure of strength. Your vantage point is invaluable. It is your *wisdom*. Dispense it generously.

Death has its place in the life cycle. The task of the elder is not simply to reaffirm life, to reinforce psychosocial strengths by maintaining meaningful involvement with people and activities. The task of the elder also includes coming to accept the inevitability of death's enforced leave-taking.

What You Can Do for Yourself and Your Family?

The notion of a personal future is openly and directly tied to the recognition that death may well not be far off, viewing the time that remains as a valuable resource.

1. Continue with all the good ideas from the other stages. More than ever, you are a valuable asset to your family.

2. Like your life; celebrate it with appreciation that you've made it to this point.

3. Get involved in ideas and activities outside yourself.

4. Find purpose in your life. Purposeful living is the best preparation for dying.

5. Remember that you are a model for your family. "Do as I say, not as I do," doesn't work. You represent the possibilities for life.

If I had any sense I'd give up, but I don't want to. I want to watch the children grow.
GREAT-GRANDMA REDHAIR, who at age 90 requires full-time care

6. Your spiritual quest will help you to integrate your experiences and to accept losses without losing heart.

7. Cultivate a positive attitude to keep your spirits high.

Everyone Rides the Carousel

We are bound by the life cycle. It is the human condition. As diverse as human experience may be, we all ride the carousel. We arrive, we travel through the stages, and we leave. Every living thing must die. By active grandparenting we extend our lives beyond our own time. The possibilities to make a difference increase with the window of opportunity in each developmental stage. Taking time with a child, encouraging the passion of a *carpe diem* attitude adds depth and meaning to our time.

Help thy brother's ship across and lo, thine own will reach the shore.

I believe that people are not seeking the meaning of life but the experience of being alive.
JOSEPH CAMPBELL

5

Family Relationships in a Changing World

Grandparents need grandchildren to keep the changing world alive for them. And grand-children need grandparents to help them know who they are and give them a sense of human experience in a world they cannot know. Here is a model of mutual learning across generations.
MARGARET MEAD

The Generation Gap

"May you live in interesting times." So says a Chinese proverb. Well, we certainly do. Interesting equals challenging. Out the window with the old view of family; you know—the mother, father, 2.3 kids and a dog, with kindly grandparents looking on. The family has changed. Grandparents are living longer, so there are more of us around to participate in our grandchildren's lives. This also means more great-grandparenting. Economic stress and higher expectations for personal fulfillment have resulted in more mothers in the workforce. Most mothers working outside the home are permanently exhausted. The increased divorce rate has cre-ated all kinds of changes: single parents, stepparents, blended families and extended families. There are more single-parent families by choice and gay couples with children. In addition, as adults who were given up for adoption at birth reconnect with their biological parents, some arrive at their birth parents with children of their own. Interfaith and interracial marriage is on the rise, and many more grandparents are full-time parents to their grandchildren. Today's family is more diverse, and it's all stressed out. Yes indeed, these are interesting times.

> After a holiday dinner at the home of my ex-husband and his wife, my husband exclaimed, "It's so good to have family!" It had been a delightfully relaxed evening. This blended family included the second wife's grandchild and her grandchild's stepsister; our daughter, son-in-law and granddaughter; and the daughter of our son's fiancée. The kids got along, the adults shared good conversation, and we all felt it was an accomplishment. Wow!

Our current information age overwhelms us with more information and stimulation than we can process. Today one *New York Times* newspaper delivers more information to us than a person living in the Middle Ages received in a lifetime. Television brings the world into our living rooms and desensitizes us to war, violence and sex. Even with careful monitoring, our grandchildren see it all. This abundance of information is having the undesirable effect of shortening their childhood. As times have changed, styles have changed, and parenting styles have changed, too.

The very basis of the family has changed, concludes a demographic report issued in 1994 by the fifteen European Union countries. The family that in the past was an institution and means of social integration has become a pact between two individuals looking for personal fulfillment.

Los Angeles Times,
July 18, 1995

A child growing up today lives with a very different reality than that of her parents and one that is worlds away from our childhood. For grandparents to adapt to these changes demands flexibility. The dual meaning of the Japanese symbol for change is *threat* and *opportunity*. It is your point of view that determines your response and shapes your experience. If you resist change because it is threatening, your response will be protective and closed. When you define change as an oppor-tunity, you are ready to openly embrace its possibilities.

Parenting is different today. It is very upsetting to see how my grandchildren are allowed to talk back to their parents. It's just not good for them. I want to protect my kids from their children, but they claim it's important for the children to express their feelings.
GRANDMA IDA BELLE

As the pace of life accelerates, the generation gap widens. Grandparents often find these changes disappointing and painful. Our values may be called into question, and adaptation may require rethinking long-held beliefs and learning to accept family situations that do not fit our expectations. On the other hand, grandparents, by virtue of experience and position, have a broader, more philosophic per-spective on life. We have an opportunity to be anchors for our family and bearers of our family's values and heritage, no matter what its size, shape or color.

There Are More of Us: Grandparents Are Living Longer

"How many Grandmas do you have?" my granddaughter's pre-school teacher asked her class.

Caitlin responded confidently, "I have seven grandmas."

"Oh, no," the teacher responded, "that's not possible."

Caitlin stuck to her guns. "I even picked out seven Mother's Day cards to send them."

The teacher was unconvinced. When Caitlin's mother came to pick her up, she con-firmed Caitlin's arithmetic, much to the teacher's amazement.

Caitlin does, indeed, have seven grand-mothers. Her four biological grandparents each have a mother living, three in their eighties and one now ninety. Caitlin knows all four of her great-grandmothers. Then there

Unfortunately, it seems very likely that the nuclear family is not a viable social form. It is too small. Each person in a nuclear family is too tightly linked to other members of the family; any one relation-ship that goes sour, even for a few hours, becomes critical; people cannot simply turn away from grandparents, grandchildren, aunts, uncles, cousins, brothers.

are two biological grandmas plus one step-grandma. Seven, count them, seven. The greater longevity of women is in evidence, for, by contrast, she has three grandfathers; one is a step-grandfather. All of her great-grandfathers are deceased, although she knew one of them. Ten grandparents in all. What a lucky little girl to know so many of her ancestors.

We are living longer. There is a senior boom underway. The group with the largest percentage increase is seniors. By the year 2030 the number of people over sixty-five will double, and by 2050 they will comprise the largest segment of the global population.

Many great-grandparents today are living active lives. Through their great-grandchildren, their lives are extended even further into the future they will never see. Great-grandparents tend to be more relaxed in their great-grandparenting role than are their children, the grandparents. Perhaps it is the wisdom of their age. Of course, there are limitations, due to the vicissitudes of age, which make them less able to be active companions or to tolerate children's noise and activity level.

An attractive, elderly couple who asked to share my table at a local coffeehouse turned out to be great-grandparents on holiday from England. "What is the difference between being grandparents and great-grandparents?" I asked.

Great-grandfather Nigel answered without hesitation: "Being a great-grandparent is more fun. First of all, I'm seventy-five now and retired, so I have more time for them. When my grandchildren were born I was working and had less time. Now, if we're asked to baby-sit and Dorothy is busy, I can do it. I'm having more fun with them than I was able to have with the grandchildren. But now it takes two of us to change a nappy [British for diaper]. You know, the babies are very active, but we have it down to a system. Dorothy holds the feet and does the cleaning up while I get the nappy, put it on and fasten it. We're more relaxed with the great-grandchildren. If the furniture gets a little scratched or the carpet a little dirty, we don't care. After all, how much longer does it have to last?"

Great-grandma Redhair, an actress, is teaching acting at the Braille Institute. "I can't believe I've lived this long. It's so much fun to see my grandchildren as parents. I love the fact that they talk things over with me and want my ideas. I'm just sorry that I don't see the little ones very often, but they live in different cities. I like to send little presents so they'll remember who I am. They like to receive money and then tell me what they've purchased. I'm blessed."

This great-grandmother enjoys the fruits of her well-established, supportive relationships with her grandchildren. She has great-grandchildren in her life, even though she's not able to see them often, a real bonus as the result of her involved grandparenting.

It's not all happy stories, however. Great-grandma Grace, who teaches an exercise class, is finding great-grandparenting difficult. "There's such a big generation gap, with so many divorces and so many on drugs. I love my great-grandson dearly but find that I have no power to protect him from a difficult life." She explained that her granddaughter was on drugs and that the boy, now six years old, was in the custody of his father and stepmother. "I've been shut out. I couldn't even get an appointment with his teacher to find out how he's doing," she complained. "I feel so frustrated and so sad."

Encouraging great-grandparents' participation in your grand-child's life is a gift of connecting them to their roots and history. Great-grandparents are living icons. They have wonderful stories to tell about a world gone by before television and automobiles. It expands the nuclear family by adding relationships. The natural affinity between grandparents and grandchildren extends to great-grandchildren enriching their experience and teaching valuable lessons on life.

Because it usually takes extra effort to arrange visits with great-grandparents and may be difficult for parents to provide this experience, it's up to you. It is an important family moment when the generations gather and is some reassurance for the prospects of aging. Go out of your way to arrange such meetings before it's too late. Remember to take your camera, video and tape recorder for this family photo-opportunity. Your family will cherish these memories.

I remember a visit to my ninety-two-year-old grandfather with my ten-year-old son, Steve. Grampa Louis was a musician who loved to sing, and Steve joined him, humming some Eastern European folk tunes. Later, at lunch, Steve became a caretaker, urging Grampa to eat, admonishing that the food would give him strength. Twenty-eight years later Steve still has fond memories of that visit.

Facilitating the great-grandparenting opportunities is not always easy and may be an extra burden, especially if you are part of the sandwich generation, the grandparents-in-the-middle. Grandparents-in-the-middle are stretched between the needs of grandchildren and kids and their responsibility to aging parents. It's called *zerrissenheit,* torn-to-pieces-hood. The stress arising from not having time for oneself is unhealthy, and it spoils the quality of life. It is vital to meet this challenge with a plan to maintain balance in your life. Without restoring yourself, you cannot be an effective caretaker for others.

The fifth day of babysitting my granddaughters (ages three and eight) was a long one. Little Raeann missed her parents and was unraveling with bursts of temper and crying. She was beyond reason because the VCR wouldn't work, and she desperately insisted on watching "Barney Goes to School." Meanwhile, I was trying to fulfill my grandparenting mission to preserve our heritage by having a Sabbath dinner. Caitie and I were trying a new chicken recipe from the Israeli cookbook she discovered in her school library. Finally, with the chicken safely in the oven, I remembered my daily check-in to my ninety-year-old mother and learned from her caretaker that she had been duped into purchasing an electric bed for five thousand dollars. So there I was in Gardenerville, Nevada, reporting this fraudulent sale to the North Hollywood Police Department, while Raeann screamed and the teenage helper watched TV. Help! Stop the carousel, I want to get off!

The good news: we did light the Sabbath candles and have what all agreed was the best chicken we'd ever tasted, and so far, mother hasn't received an electric bed. Now that I'm back home and rested I can laugh about this scene as a great example of what it's like to be in the sandwich generation.

Divorce

Few families escape the pain of divorce. The common bond grandparents already share with their grandchildren is reinforced by their common responses to divorce. Both are bystanders in this situation, impacted by events beyond their control. Their responses are similar, and they ask questions that contribute to the formation of even greater mutuality. Grandparents understand their grandchild's experience, since in many ways it mirrors their own.

If only I'd have been better. If I hadn't gotten in trouble, maybe they wouldn't be getting a divorce.

BRAD, age seven

COURTING DIVORCE

More and more couples in developed nations are ending their marriages. Divorce rates per 100 marriages:

Country	1970	1990
Canada	18.6	38.3
Czechoslovakia	21.8	32.0
Denmark	25.1	44.0
England and Wales	16.2	41.7
France	12.0	31.5
Greece	5.0	12.0
Hungary	25.0	31.0
Italy	5.0	8.0
Netherlands	11.0	28.1
Sweden	23.4	44.1
United States	42.3	54.8
(former) West Germany	12.2	29.2

Source: *Families in Focus*, by the Population Council

When faced with the reality of divorce the child asks, "What did I do wrong?" feeling somehow responsible for the breakup. The grandparent asks, "How have I failed? I must have been an inadequate parent."

Then there is anger. The child is angry that one of her parents is leaving her and may take it out on her custodial parent. "Why can't you work it out?" asks the grandparent, with a tendency to blame the in-law rather than her own child. Anxiety about the future follows. "What will happen to me?" "How will my life change?" "Have I lost my absent parent?" "Will I lose access to my grandchildren?" And then comes the sadness of the loss they both share—the loss of the family, of broken dreams.

What can grandparents do? Because divorce stirs up so many emotions, it's wise to be cautious and think before you act. Keep your own counsel to avoid overloading your children and grandchildren with your own reactions.

1. First become aware of your own feelings, especially the disappointment and anger, so that they don't pop out toward the wrong person or at the wrong place.

2. Keep in mind that you are the symbol of family stability, when all around them is caving in. Your strength is needed to shore up the family and provide a safe haven for reassurance that all is not lost.

Looking back, I know I did it all wrong when my son and daughter-in-law divorced. I let them all know how devastated I was, which burdened them and caused the very thing I was afraid of—they shut me out.

GRANDMA MADELEINE

3. Be discreet. Don't tell your grandchild all you know about the problems or all you feel about her parents' divorce. Rather, become a listening post.

4. Listen to your grandchildren without taking the side of either parent. Remember, for better or worse, your grandchild needs both parents.

5. Work to provide a positive, supportive atmosphere. This is one of the best ways to maintain access to your grandchildren.

6. Build in some fun for your grandchildren. They need a break from the tension. Help them to continue their normal lives.

Single Parenting

Although most often the result of divorce, today there are more lifestyle options being exercised and many circumstances that lead to single parenting. Whatever the reason, single parents and their children need your support.

For the approximately 30 percent of American households consisting of single adults with kids, it is an unmapped road that can lead right off an emotional cliff. They've found out the hard way that they can't have it all. Something's got to give. It's a juggling act between children, career and social life. If the children are the first priority, the social life is first to suffer. This results in social isolation and loneliness. They are in need of your love and whatever else you can give.

No one has answers to the dilemmas of single parents. It is just plain tough. Grandparents have their work cut out for them. One of the problems is that the single parent's needs are so great, grandparents find themselves feeling guilty that they're not doing enough. It is important for a grandparent to recognize that, much as you might like to, you can't make it all better. The best you can do is the best you can do. Build your relationship with your grandchildren so that they can accept the emotional support and the sense of family you provide. Everything you do is important—any financial support, large or small, such as special treats for children or parent or providing relief by taking care of the children by sitting, carpooling, cooking or doing some errands or chores and lending positive encouragement—all make a difference.

I'm so busy and so tired—and utterly without options—that I can't bother to think about my social life. My children come first.
SINGLE FATHER OF TWO

You can almost feel the single-parent struggle expressed in the poetry of a mother with two teenage daughters. This soft-spoken, fortyish artist, who works in an office by day, tells her story of broken dreams and the challenge of raising teenagers.

THE CONTEMPORARY FAMILY— IT'S A CLASSIC PLIGHT

There are three of them now,
Mother and two daughters
One, golden with light—
One dark with keen sight;
and father has long since gone.

The mother does what she can.
There's such struggle to keep unity.
It seems a classic plight;
A challenge of the century.

ANNE NORBERG

Often related to divorce and single parenting are problems about getting to see the grandchildren. When access becomes an issue, grandparents are understandably upset. Many grandparents are deprived of contact with grandchildren because the custodial parent, usually not their own child, won't allow them to visit. Due to the recognition of the importance of the grandparent-grandchild relationship, there is legal recourse in many states. Of course, a day in court does not automatically win the case, and legal action creates such expense and emotional turmoil that it should be a last resort. Consider the alternative of mediation.

Preventive measures are your first course of action. Keep your objective in mind. Divorce is highly charged with emotion, so don't be afraid to make amends with an apology, even when you don't think it fair. Here are some ideas to smooth over family disputes:

1. Examine your own behavior as objectively as you can to determine if you are part of the problem.

2. Create a climate of cooperation by not taking sides in the breakup.

3. Declare your desire to continue active grandparenting.

4. Demonstrate your good intentions by continued involvement.

5. Put your grandchildren's needs for positive grandparenting ahead of your own feelings by remaining neutral and supportive.

You gotta play the hand that is dealt you. There may be pain in that hand, but you play it.
JAMES BRADY

If these measures fail, I highly recommend mediation as a viable alternative. You can find a mediator privately or obtain one through the court. Mediators remain neutral and use a problem-solving approach to resolve family problems. When they gather the family together to talk over the issues, they seek the common ground upon which the participants can agree. This approach has helped to resolve seemingly unresolvable problems. It's amazing what a skilled mediator can accomplish. It can be a healing experience for the family and is certainly less emotionally damaging than going to court. It's also much less expensive.

Sandy and Robert sounded quite amazed as they announced they were becoming grandparents. "What's so surprising about becoming grandparents?" I asked.

"Well, we didn't expect it because none of our children are married." It turned out that their son's long-time girlfriend was expecting

It's not only what happens to you that shapes your life but how you cope with it.
ANNA FREUD

his baby. The prospective parents had no plans to live together, although their son was accepting his role as father. "We feel we're being cheated," complained the prospective grandparents. They felt a complicated mix of feelings: anger, embarrassment and excitement. Then Sandy made this wistful statement. "I've wished for years that I would have something nice to put in the church bulletin—an engagement, a wedding, a grandchild—and now we're becoming grandparents and I can't even announce it." Then she added, "My parents were very conservative people. They'd be turning over in their graves if they knew."

"How do you see your role as grandparents?" I asked.

"We just want to love this grandchild," they agreed.

The child has arrived, a girl. They flew up to see her and were thrilled. They don't enjoy easy access to the child. There's some dissension between the other grandmother and their son. But, the new grandbaby, along with her mother and father, attended Sandy and Bob's anniversary party. Sandy and Bob are determined to participate in this baby's life. They're just not sure how.

Instant Grandparenting:
Remarriage and Other Surprises

Instant grandparenting results from a variety of situations. For whatever reason it occurs, remarriage (your kids or your own), adoption or other events, it is an unexpected gift and challenge. Three key factors determine your relationship to your step-grandchild:

1. The age of the step-grandchild upon entering your life. The younger the age of the step-grandchild when you meet, the greater the chance that you will be readily accepted and have the possibility for a close relationship. Older children are less available since they are busy with schoolwork, friends and activities.

2. Who the step-grandchild lives with full-time. If the child is in the custodial care of a parent with whom you have a relationship, then naturally you will have more access and encouragement to develop your own relationship than if the child lives outside the extended family.

3. How you feel about it. Whether you find the step-grandchild appealing and want to devote your time to being a grandparent is a very personal decision. It requires time for this notion of step-grandparenting to grow on you. It is possible that you just don't feel comfortable with the child, parents or situation.

Most parents will welcome your involvement if you ask their permission and demonstrate your good intentions. Grandparenting step-grandchildren can be successful, but not if you pretend that they are just like biological grandchildren. You must first become friends. When you are able to open your heart and give of yourself, rewards follow.

An example of what a stepparent, or any parent, should avoid was told by Meridith, a vibrant forty-year-old single mom with a five-year-old daughter. "It is very annoying that my new stepmother, who has no children of her own, criticizes my parenting," she complained. "She feels that the patience and consideration I show my five-year-old daughter is indulgent. I've tried to explain my views, but she's not concerned with feelings and has a very authoritarian point of view. She is certainly not an authority on the subject. It's hard enough to be a single parent, and her judgments spoiled our visit to their house." By voicing her opinions, this stepmother is risking her future relationship with her new family and turning her stepdaughter away. Meridith confided that she was going to try to avoid her stepmother and see her dad alone. This is an example of how little is accomplished by voicing criticism.

My own story with instant grandparenting began when my bachelor son phoned to make his annual request for help with Christmas gift wrapping.

"Sure," I replied, "Come on over."

Then he ventured, a bit tentatively, "May I bring a little girl I'm baby-sitting?"

"Of course. See you in a little bit."

This breezy little conversation was not nearly as casual as it sounds. The gift to be wrapped was for my son's new girlfriend (I had heard from his sister that he was seeing someone), and the little girl was her five-and-a-half-year-old daughter. I must admit that my first thoughts when I heard about the child were not joyous. After all, marrying into a ready-made family is more complicated than starting from scratch.

Steve is a very private person, and the fact that he was including me in his personal life was significant. I was about to participate in his courtship by wrapping my potential daughter-in-law's gift (you can be sure I did a deluxe job of it), and I was about to meet a possible grandchild. This is not everyday stuff. What would she be like? Would she be appealing, or a kid I would have to learn to tolerate? What kind of emotional baggage would she carry? After all, she's the product of a divorce (that's the therapist in me). Most important of all, would she like me?

I was startled by the doorbell, took a deep breath, and tried my best to appear offhand. There they were, my bachelor son with a child! Gulp . . . that takes some time getting use to. What a sudden change. A beautiful, shining face was smiling at me. Eloise was a dream, and Steve was obviously enjoying his potential new role. He'll make a good dad. It looked good. I had lucked out. I could only hope her mother was as delightful. She is.

Steve and Eloise's mom were married a few months later, and Papa and Grandma Lilly (our names had already been established by our first grandchild) became instant grandparents. There are a lot of adjustments. And, yes, there is baggage from the past. I can honestly say I love this child, and I do believe she's happy I'm her grandma. We've had good times and some heart-to-heart talks. But a year and a half later she still won't call me Grandma Lilly. I'd really like her to, but her reluctance is a reminder that it takes time.

Cathy's remarriage was to Alan, who has three children from his first marriage. Cathy has a daughter, Marisa. Gammy and Donny, Cathy's mother and stepfather, have become instant grandparents to Alan's three kids. They have embraced them, along with Alan's mother and stepfather. But, of course, their relationship to the children in not like the one they have with Marisa, who is a blood relative and whose life they've participated in from the beginning. I'm on the other side of the family so that, occasionally, we come together with Cathy's new family. It makes for a greatly extended family that works pretty well, especially if you have a big house. The secret is acceptance. All these kids need love and attention. The more caring grandparents they have around them, the better. Be one of those.

The Past Returns: Crisis or Opportunity?

"Guess what! I have another sister," a thirty-something friend announced.

"What do you mean, another sister?" I asked. He already had three, and his mother is sixty.

"Well, it seems that forty years ago while Mom was in college, she had a daughter who she gave up for adoption."

"Did you know about this?"

"No, nobody did, not even Dad."

"Have you met her?"

"Not yet, but she's coming for my youngest sister's wedding with her husband and her two kids."

"How do you feel about it?" I asked.

"I'm digesting it. I'm digesting it," he said thoughtfully.

This situation is being repeated in many households as more adopted children seek their biological parents. The reactions are mixed. A found mother I'll call Sally was angry. She had been assured that she could not be traced and did not want to be found. She felt that the appearance of this child ruined her life. Simon, a nineteen-year-old adoptee, was given a cool reception by his biological family, who clearly couldn't make room for him in their lives. I've also heard other positive stories about family celebrations held for newcomers.

The reappearance of a long-lost child has different meanings to the various participants in this real-life drama. For the brothers and sisters, it changes their view of reality. They may experience a sense of betrayal over this long-held secret. In the first story, for example, the oldest sister harbors a lot of anger toward her mother, who was so strict with her about premarital sex. Their birth order is instantly changed, the first child is no longer the first, and sibling rivalry is revived. Even grown-up children resent a newcomer taking up Mom and Dad's time. And what about inheritance? Is the newcomer included in the will? A big question mark hovers over the family. It also serves as a reminder that their parent is not perfect and is a sexual being—very uncomfortable feelings that are filled with value judgments. Somehow we tend to preserve the silly notion that our parents don't do such things.

For the parent who experiences this return from the past, this child represents a hidden shame, a lifelong secret now out of the bag. The parents' marriage is challenged by the new reality. However, there is relief with disclosure and openness, and there is joy over the return of a child one has longed for, wondered about and suffered guilt over. Perhaps the easiest part is accepting the new grandchildren. Particularly if they are young, they seem to be above the fray of emotions. The other grandchildren, the new cousins, seem to be more accepting than the adult children to embrace a new sibling. Their reactions will be strongly influenced by those of their parents, whose lead they will ultimately follow.

Grandma Evelyn felt threatened by her adopted daughter Marta's biological mother. Marta sought and found her biological mother when she was married in her twenties with her own little girl. Evelyn was heartbroken and felt she must now compete for her daughter's and granddaughter's love. She was threatened by the fact that the biological mother could afford more lavish gifts. She was fearful that her daughter and granddaughter would pre-fer the newly surfaced biological mother, especially since her rela-tionship with her daughter had been rocky. This is a story filled with heartache, without an easy ending.

Another story of complications in family life and instant grandparenting is less than pretty. When her mother's heretofore unknown son and his family appeared, Emily, the forty-year-old daughter, was propelled into psychotherapy to help her sort it all out. Although her mother sees her new family from time to time, she's not very involved in their lives.

These situations require time, time, more time, patience, and a lot of talking with other members of the family. There are no quick solutions. This process, like digestion, can't be hurried. Other family members don't necessarily experience the joy of the return of this child that you may. Your response sets the example for the rest of the family. At any rate, it's a highly personal and highly emotional event that, by its nature, becomes a family event. You can hope that the family will embrace their new member with open arms, but realistically it's unpredictable; so be patient. Remain patient and sensitive to the reactions of others, and don't force it.

Whether your newly arrived family presents you with a crisis or an opportunity, you've got your work cut out for you. Grandparenthood, by whatever means, requires acceptance and consideration of the other family members. In situations like these, the grandchildren will benefit by special attention. The bottom line: keep communication open.

Alternative Lifestyles

Gay and Lesbian Couples

Many parents have worked hard to open their hearts to their gay or lesbian children, but when they become more public by forming a family with children, it is yet another challenge. If you are unable to support this lifestyle, either work at it with some form of therapy or get out of the way. Society makes it difficult enough for couples living alternative lifestyles. Don't add to it. If this is a struggle for you, I hope you will find it in your heart to rejoice that your child has enriched her/his life with love and the blessing of children. They deserve all you can give. You have everything to gain by being a proud and involved grandparent.

A gay friend I'll call Howard was proudly showing off photos of his twin sons. His story is testimony to medical science and social change. "I never thought about fatherhood. It just wasn't in the cards," he said with a smile. "But when my gay sister and her partner decided to have a child, they asked if I would donate my sperm to my sister's partner, to give their baby the closest possible biological match to themselves."

God give us grace to accept with serenity the things that cannot be changed, courage to change the things which should be changed, and the wisdom to distinguish the one from the other.

REINHOLD NIEBUHR

"How does your mom feel about all of this?" I asked.

"Well, she's more excited than any of us," Howard reported. "With two homosexual children, she never dreamed she'd be a grandmother. It's a real gift."

They have become an uncommon and loving family, proof of social change.

Interfaith/Interracial Families

It's not exactly what you planned; your child has married into a different faith, culture or race. Interfaith, interracial and intercultural marriages introduce a whole range of questions and issues that were simply not relevant to most grandparents in previous generations. The first question posed to such mixed-marriage couples is, "What about the children?" It's true that when children are involved, these marriages present new questions to parents and grandparents alike regarding the child's identity and beliefs. Most couples must struggle to find their way.

Grandparents have a very definite contribution to make here as the link to their faith and culture. Developing children's religious, racial and cultural identity provides

The best way of learning is through difference.

CATHERINE MEAD-BATESON

them with the building blocks for their identity, the knowledge of who they are. It gives them a sense of belonging to something greater than themselves. When you teach your grandchildren about your unique heritage, you are telling them about yourself. It's a way for them to get to know you. Grandparents have a right to tell their grandchildren who they are, with the parents' permission. When this is done in a nonjudgmental way, you can have a tremendous positive influence.

First of all, face your own feelings and prejudices about the differences. The degree of difficulty this presents depends on deep-seated beliefs. Today we are learning the value of embracing diversity. It enriches our lives. You must proceed with great diplomacy so that you don't offend the parents when transmitting your grandchildren's heritage, by carefully considering what you say and how you say it. By accepting differences, you can bring harmony to the family and nurture mutual respect and love in the midst of ambiguity. Because of the high divorce rate, members of the same household or extended family may include four or five different religions or cultures. This creates a situation that requires great tolerance and a need to appreciate and respect differences. It is a rich learning opportunity.

"The 8 x 10 photograph of my parents' wedding occupies a prominent place in both the living room of my house and the recesses of my mind. A record of the pivotal event in the lives of my father and mother, it also signifies my striking diverse heritage. In the middle of the nuptial scene stand my parents, with my uncles and aunts, now long since gray, and grandparents, some since gone, at their side. To my father's right, the group is Minneapolis Conservative Jews, three generations removed from Russia, one generation removed from poverty. My grandfather, stern as always, beckons me to persevere as he did. Grandpa supported his entire family from age twelve, when he peddled papers on the freezing corners of St. Paul for nickels and dimes. He exudes the satisfaction of having raised both himself and others up, but grimaces as if to tell me that the fight is far from over. To the left of my mother, the wedding participants are Black Baptists from Bennettsville, South Carolina. They stare fiercely into my eyes, urging me to carry on a tradition forged with sweat, toil, and pride in the cotton field and the pulpit."

JONAH MARTIN EDELMAN

Remember:

1. Respect the parents' authority, and don't go against their wishes.

2. Parents are their children's teachers; grandparents are their philosophy teachers.

3. Celebrate holidays and make them a continuing tradition. This is a wonderful way to introduce your beliefs and customs.

We must continue to allow difference until difference doesn't matter any more.
JOHNNETTA COLE
President, Spelman College

4. Don't forget the importance of food, music and stories. Food offers the flavor of your culture; music captures a culture's emotions; stories offer lessons to ponder and stir the imagination. Be creative!

5. Of course you prefer your own faith and culture, but don't undermine your grandchild's self-esteem by talking against the other side.

6. In the spirit of celebrating your families' diversity, include your in-law child in your discussions and celebrations.

7. You are the standard-bearer for your grandchild's faith and culture. The way you honor and celebrate for yourself is an example of your beliefs. Your actions speak louder than words.

I bring the Passover celebration to my granddaughter each year, even bringing some ingredients with me on the plane. You can imagine my delight that she considers it her favorite holiday. I involve her in the preparations, so we have fun together. It's so satisfying to know that I am providing an experience she would not otherwise enjoy and that she has developed a positive identification with this part of her heritage. Fortunately it's made easier because her father, Craig, who is of a different faith, is very accepting and gets into the spirit of the celebration, too.

Grandparents Raising Grandchildren

Talk about mixed feelings, this takes the cake. There are 3.4 million grandparents in the United States raising their kids' kids. This number increased 40 percent in three years. These grandparents are assuming the parental responsibilities for their grandchildren as a result of their adult children's inability to care for their own children. Stepping in to rescue a grandchild, they have taken on the parental role once again. Only this second time around they are older and less energetic, albeit wiser.

President Clinton's grandparents raised him until he was four. Their pictures hung in his office in Little Rock when he was Arkansas governor. Clinton has urged older Americans to act as surrogate grandparents for children who have none.

Assuming the constant demands of childrearing requires grandparents to set aside their own pursuits and plans; it is really an heroic act that often feels to them like a giant step backward. A malfunction in the family precipitates the need for a grandparent to take over as parent. Most often, the situation springs from a teenage pregnancy or a child's involvement in substance abuse, although there are other factors such as illness, economic hardship, incarceration and death. Instead of the joyful anticipation of expectant parenthood, grandparents begin their task in the climate of an undesirable and stressful event. Usually it is precipitated by a desperate need to rescue the grandchild from inadequate parenting and foster care.

Grandparents who have undertaken the parenting of a grandchild are often disappointed and angry about being deprived of their grandparent status, yet relieved that they are finally in charge. The concerns of daily care preempt the usual freedom that grandparents enjoy. Parenting grandparents experience a gamut of emotions, from frustration and anger to disappointment and sadness, due to the problems surrounding this need and to the complex emotions around their own situation as they reckon with what they must give up in their own lives in favor of the demands of childrearing. It disrupts the relationship between grandparents and can set them at odds with each other. All of this changes their life expectations. Of course the complications are combined with the satisfaction that they are doing the best for their grandchildren and the joy that children can bring.

When grandparents must take over, they often experience a sense of failure, believing that their own imperfect parenting makes them responsible for the problems. Financial hardships bear down on these grandparents, forcing them to reduce their time at work and requiring them to stretch their often limited retirement incomes. Unfortunately, grandparents who have taken over the care of grandchildren are not eligible for financial grants or aid as foster parents, although they are serving in that capacity. Many grandparents who have found themselves in this boat are fighting for legislation that would recognize their situation by providing the relief of financial aid. [See Resources for Grandparents.]

Raising my grandson is hard. I have no time on my own to relax, and it's physically harder than the first time.

Life experience has left these grandchildren with emotional scars that make them challenging to raise. They are often fearful, angry or depressed and have behavior problems. Fathers are generally not in the picture, and if they are, it's usually only for occasional visits. There's little support for the grandparent-parent. Conflicts arise between mothers and daughters over how to raise *their* child. The mother-adult-daughter relationship, a complicated association in the best of times, is fraught with an undercurrent of emotions. The mother's disappointment with her adult child is compounded by her guilt feelings that she is to blame for the problems. The adult child's unresolved resentments and tendency to blame her parents for her own predicament is coupled with her sense of inadequacy and failure. Because children take time and energy and resources before they give back any gratification to their caretakers, most grandparents who are parenting their grandchildren find satisfaction in the knowledge that they are providing the best possible life for these children. Support groups for grandparents raising grandchildren provide a forum for their many issues.

At my age I never thought I'd be bringing up kids.

GRANDMOTHER whose daughter is a drug addict

When Grandparents Divorce

Although still in the minority, today older people are more willing to end unsatisfactory marriages. The number of couples seeking new alternatives and more interesting lives through divorce in their fifties and later is on the rise. When grandparents divorce, their adult children are affected. Their symbol of family solidarity crumbles. Parents divorcing may also revive an adult child's early feelings of abandonment. The stability of a family place is threatened. Suddenly they feel homeless. They can't go home. Home will never be the same. Holidays and celebrations will never be the same. With this in mind, follow these guidelines:

— Reassure your grandchildren that you will still be there for them and that you will continue to do things together. Talk to them without burdening them with your troubles.

— Don't be divisive by talking against your spouse. It further weakens the family.

— Avoid putting your kids in the middle by refusing to be at the same gathering as your ex.

— Plan time with your family, especially with the grandchildren. They can provide a respite from the fray and nourishment at this time of uncertainty in your life.

— Don't expect your family and grandchildren to provide a life for you.

— Do whatever you can to maintain a positive attitude about life; you are still a model for your family. Recognize that transitions are always challenging and that things do get better.

Special-Needs Grandchildren

Lacking the close support of expanded families, friendly neighborhoods and stable communities, the special needs of *special children* should earn our special attention. They are especially vulnerable in today's market-driven and socially fractured society, and the data reveal that those classified broadly as developmentally disabled are routinely disadvantaged. This includes children who are physically and mentally disabled, emotionally disturbed, learning disabled—as with Attention Deficit Disorder (ADD)—crack babies, and a wide circle of those who are simply culturally retarded (children who are behind in social skills and deprived of cultural experiences).

In spite of the Americans with Disabilities Act and many efforts to recognize and serve the needs of those who are handicapped, the social safety net in public education and in family services is under assault in a downsizing economy. Children are among those on the street. The opportunity for grandparent service has never been greater.

Parents of children with special needs require assistance and relief. They are worn out by the day-to-day care and worry. The testimony of a young woman patient who endured the trauma of sexual harassment is a powerful reminder of the special need for grandparents. Often the needy one can develop more comfortably with the grandparents, outside the anxiety-provoking relationship with mother and father.

As a mentally handicapped child, Cindy grew up in a loving family that gave her the opportunity to develop and work and live independently. After months of sexual harassment in her workplace, she mustered the courage to tell her family and seek relief. Her response to my question, "Did you feel like fighting back when you were harassed?" made her courage more evident. When I commended her courage and asked where it came from, she replied, "From my grandmother, who always understood me." We agreed that her grandmother, now deceased, would be very proud of her.

A lawyer friend told me that he and his wife had no family to help or encourage them or their permanently bedridden son. "We are just worn out by the demands of our work and family and long for the input of grandparents."

Meanwhile Grandma Alma is making a major contribution to her family and, in turn, is comforted by their close proximity since her husband died. She lives in her own quarters on the property with her daughter and son-in-law and three grandchildren. Toby, the middle child, has cerebral palsy and requires total care. Grandma has a special relationship with Toby and understands his language. She assists with his care. By relieving the parents, she allows them to have some normalcy in their lives—such as outings with each of their children—and even to get away for vacations.

DOs AND DON'Ts

1. DO embrace change as an opportunity.

2. DO promote interaction between great-grandparents and great-grandchildren. The elders are living ancestors. They provide a living history lesson.

3. DO manage to make time for yourself by setting priorities, particularly if you're a grandparent sandwiched in the middle between grandchildren, children and aging parents.

4. DO utilize the common reactions to divorce you share with your grandchild to help develop understanding and empathy with her.

5. DON'T openly take sides in a divorce, for you could be the loser by losing access to your grandchildren. Instead, listen, listen, listen.

6. DO help out the single parent, but don't become intrusive.

7. DO give your step-grandchildren love and care. In order to succeed in their lives, all children need to have an adult who believes in them, and you may be that one.

8. DO remember that you have a definite contribution to make in interfaith, interracial or intercultural marriages, for you are the bridge to your own faith, race and culture. The grandchildren are not one or the other. Their identity includes all of their genetic history.

9. DO celebrate diversity.

10. DO make special-needs grandchildren feel special.

6

Long-Distance Grandparenting

"Teach me how to be a better long-distance grandparent," a grandmother pleaded. "It's the greatest heartache of my life, being far away from my grandchildren."

If you feel cheated because your grandchildren don't live nearby, take heart. Being a long-distance grandparent doesn't mean you can't have a significant relationship with your grandchildren and play an important role in their lives. It's true, you do miss the day-to-day contact—you won't run into them in the supermarket or be able to pick them up at school—but long-distance grandparenting can be vital and rewarding. It does take effort, planning and organization. It's a bit like waging your own public relations campaign and finding various ways that will reach beyond the superficial to learn about them and tell them about yourself. The key to long-distance relationships is keeping in touch creatively and being consistent.

"You never know how you influence your grandchildren," said Grandmere Odile. "You are their spiritual director. Grandparents are not irritated by events of every day. They have a larger view and more patience. As two working parents, my daughter and son-in-law are too stressed and become impatient.

"I have three grandchildren (ages seven, thirteen and eighteen), all living in France. I try to visit them once a year. My grandson was going to double his class [repeat seventh grade]. His father was so upset and felt that it was bad and that his son would be late starting college. I had many conversations with my grandson. I encouraged him. I pointed out that this delay is nothing compared to the length of his life. He visited me that summer for one month. He lives in the country, so on this visit he discovered other people living different ways and learned that's okay. He started to change after that summer. Today he's first in his class. I know I made a difference and changed his life."

Establish Your Relationship by Keeping in Touch

Out of sight, out of mind.

In order to strengthen your ties, you must keep sending reminders. You must make sure to be there in spirit. It will be helpful to be organized with a list of important dates such as birthdays, recitals and other occasions, so when you're unable to attend these events you can still be involved by phone, fax, email, card or gift. These are opportunities to stay close. Stimulate your creative juices with the following thoughts for communication.

Happiness is not getting what you like but liking what you get.

Keeping in Touch by Telephone

Just as the ad suggests, you can *reach out and touch someone*. Telephone calls are probably the easiest and most spontaneous way to do it. It's so satisfying to share the latest news while it's fresh and to hear those beautiful voices. However, long-distance calls do get expensive, and conversation with kids is not always successful. Your grandchild may be wonderfully talkative, yet sometimes, regardless of age, a telephone conversation may be limited and superficial, reduced to monosyllables like: "How are you?" "Fine." "How is school?" "Okay."

On my seventy-fifth birthday, the calls from the grandchildren made me give thanks for the past and take hope for the future. I am determined to stay healthy and grow old with them.

PAPA SAM

Here are some guidelines for telephone relationships:

1. They're never too young to listen to your voice. I recently sang "Happy Birthday" to my one-year-old granddaughter Raeann. My son-in-law reported that she listened and smiled.

2. Be considerate. If you make your call at what happens to be an inconvenient time, be willing to hang up and call another time. Some grandparents like to have a regular, prearranged time for calls. I find spontaneity more successful.

3. Learn how to keep the conversation going with young children who do not have the gift of gab by asking specific, concrete questions you might have in mind. Who did you play with today? What did you have for dinner? Did you like it?

4. Avoid the pitfall of taking sides in family disagreements. My seven-year-old granddaughter telephoned me when she was upset with her dad.

   "Do you know what your son just did?" she asked. "He told me I could have my Game Boy on the weekend, and now it's the weekend and he won't let me have it."

   "Why not?" I asked.

   "I don't know," she answered.

   Fortunately I recognized that this was an invitation to get in the middle of a family problem and didn't bite. I was sympathetic to her plight but counseled that she needed to talk to him and find out why he wouldn't let her have her toy. I offered my assistance to facilitate their discussion if needed. Well, I never heard about it again. Obviously, she knew she was on thin ice and was seeking an ally. I was flattered that she turned to me but relieved that I had avoided that booby trap. It just goes to show that even a long-distance grandparent can interfere and stir up trouble.

5. Let them know you by telling them about yourself and what you are thinking or doing—simple everyday things like what you had for breakfast, what you saw on your walk, what you read in the paper, or how you feel when you play tennis.

6. Be a sympathetic listener, showing respect for your grandchild's feelings. It will encourage her to confide in you.

7. Facilitate a problem-solving approach without reprimand. Encourage dreams and share ideas. This is how your own philosophy of life is revealed.

8. Be aware that telephone conversations can teach communication skills.

9. Organize a family conference call to bring all together to say, "Happy Birthday," or, "Susan is expecting a baby," or even a sad message, such as, "Grampa may die tomorrow."

10. Video conferences are the newest innovation for family communication. It takes organization and is expensive. By gathering the family at a video conference center to communicate with long-distance family gathered in another city (even another country, just like those hookups you see on national television), you can create a space-age family reunion.

Although hearing a family member's voice does bridge the miles, when the receiver is returned to its cradle, you are left with good feelings but nothing tangible in hand. For that reason, other forms of communication that provide concrete evidence of your connection should be added to your repertoire, such as letters, email, faxes, tape recordings, videos and the high-tech video-telephones. Email is growing in popularity as an avenue for keeping in touch. It is easy, fast, inexpensive and very convenient (you don't have to worry about timing or time zones). I urge you to push yourself to participate in this technology.

The Lost Art of Letter Writing

A letter is a gift, a wonderfully personal gift that is a lasting memory. Letter writing is practically a lost art and worth rediscovering. First of all, it's thrilling for your grandchild to receive a letter addressed to her. Then, it stirs a sense of anticipation. What message will it hold? Receiving mail is guaranteed to make the recipient feel special at any age.

As a form of communication, letters have many advantages. They are a lasting memento. A saved letter is like a time machine. Reading it over and over again allows us to travel back in time. A letter is personal—a gift of yourself expressing your point of view in your own words. When you effectively impart your thoughts and ideas, you are making an intimate connection, which is therapeutic for the writer.

Biographers and historians rely on information found in letters to reconstruct history, for they chronicle the history of time and place. What better way to document your family history for your grandchildren? Tell stories about your experiences, about your own childhood and their parents' childhood. To make sure your letters are saved, provide a box or scrapbook for them.

Request that your letter be answered. The responsibility to answer a letter requires discipline. It's a good learning experience and encourages the development of valuable skills. Younger children can dictate their words or draw a picture. For older children it's an exercise in articulating their thoughts and feelings, developing vocabulary, spelling and penmanship.

Morandi has always sent me drawings. They say more than words could possibly say.
PAPA SAM

Another kind of letter that is worth saving is the picture-word letter for young children. Pictures are used in lieu of words. A picture of a deer is part of your salutation, for example. It becomes a creative project.

You don't have to abandon communication by mail, even if you don't have time for letters. Send cards, postcards, newspaper and magazine clippings, a beautiful leaf, a licorice stick or any number of things you will think of yourself.

Random Acts of Kindness

Practicing random acts of kindness just because you feel like it sends a message: "I'm thinking of you." It may be some stickers, a dollar bill, a newspaper article, a book, some socks, a hair-band or a special treat you've made. You can also introduce a new idea in the form of an article or book. You can send along something that lets them know you know what they're up to these days—a can of tennis balls, for example, or a pair of ballet tights. Whatever your choice, you are building a bridge across the distance.

Tape Recordings

Hearing your voice is music to your family's ears. It makes you a familiar presence. Talk a letter into your tape recorder. Although it may seem awkward at first, you will quickly get over any self-consciousness so it becomes just like having an ordinary conversation. Receiving such a tape is a family event. You can encourage a "talk by tape" correspondence. I have a treasured tape recording of my daughter Carrie when she was three years old. Hearing that sweet little voice transports me to another era. It amuses her and amazes her daughter.

When you read a favorite story to your grandchild on tape, she can have time with you whenever she wants. You might send the book with the tape, so she can follow along. These tape recordings become family heirlooms.

Visual Reminders

Photos are always welcome and lasting reminders that become part of the family's archives. Having photos of us in the grand-child's house gives us a presence in their lives. Our image is impressed upon them when it is seen regularly. Photos taken of your everyday activities will make a little album about grandma and grandpa and a statement about your lives. Grandma Ida and Grandpa Jack made an album from photos taken of them throughout a typical day for their teenage grandson. This record has become even more valuable to him now that both of them have died.

A chronicle of your travels shares your experiences. I usually document my visit to the grandchildren or their visit to me with a little album of photos as a reminder of our time together.

Put a picture of yourself in a frame so it can easily be displayed and won't end up in a drawer.

Video yourself talking to the children, reading to them, show-ing them things you want to share. Giving a video camera to your long-distance family helps to ensure that you will have videos of them. Actually seeing them in action is a great way to have a little visit when you're missing them. A picture is worth a thousand words.

Scrapbooks and Collections

My friend Charlotte describes the scrapbooks her grandmother made for her as magical. Somehow, those pictures cut from maga-zines and pasted onto the large manila pages offered her a sense of life's possibilities. Scrapbooks can be made about anything you like; you might develop a theme, e.g., cars, flowers, animals, or the extended family. Postcards provide interesting pictures and can be slipped easily into photo albums.

By sharing an interest or hobby, you engage in an activity together. A stamp or coin collection gives you something to talk about, and as you send additions to the collection you also contribute to your connection. Cultivate interests in common and build on them together: sports, politics, gardening. Steve and his Grandpa Joe enjoyed sports together, watched games together and kept in close touch to talk over, celebrate or complain about their favorite teams. I always felt there was a deeper message in their communication.

Mind Trips

Reality is what we create with our minds.

When you go on an outing, take your grandchild with you. How? By using your imagination. When I take my morning walk, I carry on an imaginary conversation with my grandchild Caitie. Sound a little crazy? Well, try it; you may like it. I mentally put words to my thoughts, commenting about the birds, cloud formations, or the ocean and how I feel. I've found that this has the added advantage of heightening my awareness of my surroundings and makes me feel close to her. Once home, I dash off a note telling her about our walk. I draw little pictures to illustrate my story. (I'm no artist, but she doesn't mind that my water bird looks more like a turkey.) I fax it to her, so she gets it immediately. It gives me a feeling of connection. I'm told she greets her daddy in the evening with the news, "This is what the beach looked like today." (P.S. I'm saving the originals in a binder for her.)

Holidays

Celebrating holidays together is an opportunity to deepen their meaning, especially when you add your cultural flavoring. Foods and rituals provide a vehicle for family experience. Special occasions give us a chance to shine. We keep traditions and create new ones. Teaching the family traditions and developing new ones lets the family know they are a family unit; they have roots.

There's another side to holidays. They bring painful reminders of absence, of who's missing, of bygone family gatherings, of loss, separation and divorce. They may also highlight differences of age, of place, of religious faith and ritual—Hanukkah and Christmas— the distance of South Dakota and Nevada and Southern California. Grandparents can play an essential role as healers, mending broken relationships; they can close the family circle.

Uncle David becomes a part of the celebration by making Caitie a birthday crown each year. Last year, at her request, it featured a galloping horse; this year it sparkled with golden jewels.

If you can't be together on a special occasion, devise a way to be represented. Send food or special treats. It's best if you make them. You might make ornaments to add to the decor or send a message to be read or heard when all are gathered. By adding to the festivities, you escape being forgotten; you are there.

Bridging the Generation Gap

It's not always easy to keep up with a child when you don't see her on a regular basis. Grandchildren grow and change so fast that you risk becoming an outsider. I realized the value of hands-on experience with a child similar in age to my granddaughter, who lives in another city, quite by accident. A young patient of mine happened to be just her age. My time with her kept me in touch with how kids are at that age—the physical development and changes, the interests, vocabulary and vantage point of five-year-olds. Lack of knowledge creates gaps between you that makes you less compatible. You can narrow that gap by contact with children close to your long-distance grandchildren's ages.

Begin to notice the children you see in your daily life at the supermarket, restaurant or church and observe their behavior. If you are so inclined, you can befriend grandchildren of friends, ask to be included on an outing, or take the child on an outing. By extending your grandparenting you are extending your influence. You may want to attend a school program or volunteer to tutor children or assist the teacher.

Grandparenting for the Greater Good

Clyde Forde does some of the most important work in Boston. Every morning, he gathers up all the caring he has amassed over seventy-eight years and delivers it to children who need it. Since he retired from Westinghouse he has participated in the national Foster Grandparent Program.

"From the time I was a little kid, I wanted to be a doctor," he says in his lilting Barbados accent. "My life has taken different turns. But deep within, I always had this feeling that I wanted to help children. I see an honesty in them I don't see in big people." The doctors clearly value Forde and often call upon him to calm the children during examinations and ask for his input. Asked how many foster grandchildren he has had over the years, Forde, who has four grandchildren of his own, chuckles. "You couldn't even count them."

EDITH SARAH STEIN, *A Time for Every Purpose*

The Foster Grandparent Program in the schools needs you, and so do the children's programs at your church or synagogue, the children's museum or zoo, or youth groups such as Girls Incorporated or the YMCA. Your community needs you; children need you. With the existing age-segregation we have lost connections to our essential role as elders and the richness it gives us and the children. We have a valuable contribution to make that is no longer built into the social fabric. Hands-on experience with children not only gives us a greater understanding of our own grandchildren, it is a recognition of our essential role.

So many kids don't know their grandparents. . . .
FOSTER GRANDPARENT PROGRAM

Your Visit

Keep your visits special by keeping them brief (rule of thumb is three days). There is an old show business adage that says, "Leave them wanting more." Ending a visit while everyone is still enjoying it works for everyone. It fosters good feelings and happy memories and makes them want you to come back.

If you are staying longer, be aware of your intrusion in family routines. You have a tricky role as both the parent/caretaker and guest. Make certain to be a helpful member of the family without just taking over; ask permission before you act. It's not your house, so be respectful of your hosts, and don't criticize. Remember the old Frank Sinatra song "My Way"? Well, you can't have it.

By all means, bring presents—something thoughtful, not necessarily expensive. Perhaps it can be something for a project you can do together, like a new cookie recipe and cookie cutter for a baking project, plans and materials to build a bird house, a book that introduces a subject you enjoy.

Make your time special by planning an outing. Take the family out for a meal, buy a special treat for dinner, or cook a favorite meal. Don't forget that your visit is an opportunity to give the parents some relief. You might offer to babysit and let the parents have a night out or even an overnight. Some grandparents I know give a regular anniversary present of a night in a hotel while they babysit. The added advantage is that it allows you to have the children to yourself.

Don't miss this opportunity to pass on cultural and family traditions. You might plan your trip around a particular celebration or holiday and help provide the meal and ritual around it. I arrive each Passover to shop for and prepare the holiday meal. Then I conduct the Seder service for my daughter's family. It has become my granddaughter's favorite holiday and one she would not have without my participation. Of course, I couldn't do this without her parents' blessing. Bring pictures of family, perhaps of Mom or Dad when they were the grandchildren's ages. Bring music in any form. Cook meals that link you to your cultural background and tell stories that underscore meaning. Tell stories about when Mom or Dad were little. Celebrate. Make your visit a special occasion.

Don't Forget Your Kids

Extend your TLC to your kids. They're never too old to need care from their mom and dad. Of course, they enjoy a special present, too. A great way to support today's stressed-out family is to do odd jobs around the house, with their blessing of course. When Grandma Libby comes for her extended visit each summer she cleans drawers and cupboards and organizes the household. Grandpa Bob brought his roto-tiller and cultivated the garden for spring planting. Grandma Janis bakes up a storm for the freezer; Papa Sam, an architect, designed the decking for the hot tub. I usually make some soups for the freezer, check on the children's schooling by observing their classrooms, and offer a bit of child development information when asked. Take photos to document your visit and make them into a little story book or album. Plant something in the garden. They can eat the carrots Grandpa planted weeks after you've gone. I'm sure you get the idea. Let the memory of your visit linger by leaving something behind.

Because of distance, your input is at a premium. You're not a natural part of their day, so whatever you do takes on added value. If you give up your efforts and drift away, your children lose a vital connection, and so do you.

DOs AND DON'Ts

1. DON'T let distance defeat you.

2. DO call on modern technology to keep in touch.

3. DO become a fax or email family.

4. DO arrange and keep records of significant events.

5. DO let the children help to make the holiday.

6. DO travel on senior coupons and take advantage of senior travel plans. You'll be able to see them more often.

7. DO prepare for a visit by sending a honey-baked ham ahead of your arrival. The kids may not have time to cook.

8. DO think of meeting them halfway at places you have never visited.

9. DO send boxes of food to your grandchild away at school or in military service.

10. DON'T be too disappointed if thank-you letters are not forthcoming.

11. DO celebrate small events.

12. DO make geography lessons out of moves and visits.

7

Over the River and Through the Wood . . .

Over the river and through the wood, to grandfather's house we go. . . .

Don't those words fill you with the warmth and glow of family togetherness? Isn't that what we all dream of, a close-knit, happy family? It looks
so easy on television, so picture-perfect as family members laugh and hug,
and the turkey is never dry. But is this real life? No, it's not. This is an ide-
alized version of family life that, if used as a
measure of your own experience, is bound to
lead to disappointment. Families are made up

*A family is judged by how
well they don't get along.*

of real people—real people who are much more complex than those on TV,
real people who are not perfect and don't resolve their problems in a half-
hour time slot. Perfect is a dangerous standard. Sometimes the turkey is dry.

> *Over the river and through the wood,*
> *to grandfather's house we go;*
> *The horse knows the way*
> *To carry the sleigh,*
> *Through the white and drifted snow.*

131

Over the river and through the wood
When grandmother sees us come,
She will say "Oh Dear,
The children are here,
Bring a pie for everyone."
We will kiss them all
And play snowball
And stay as long as we can.

"Flowers for Children"

Every family has its conundrums. It's not always easy to get along, and sometimes the kids act just plain awful. By idealizing others you depreciate your own experience. Believing that all those other families are without flaws is bound to make you feel that yours is deficient by comparison.

A realistic view of family will actually help you to enjoy them more and will encourage acceptance of inevitable imperfections. It's also a reminder to savor those special moments that may approach your ideal.

Expectations shape our experiences, for better or for worse. I am reminded of a story I heard from a woman who had an arranged marriage. She did not know her husband prior to their marriage. "As a new bride I had no expectations for romance," she explained. "I just prayed that my groom would have some redeeming qualities and would be bearable. I was so grateful for each positive attribute I found. It has worked out well." She continued, "The American way of romance expects everything and then becomes more and more disillusioned with the relationship." Although I am not advocating arranged marriages, this example of how expectations shape experience certainly speaks to the inherent disadvantage of romantic expectations.

In their role as human tranquilizers, the best grandparents exert their wise influence by remote control, never letting on that the parents are merely following the subtle commands of vastly superior beings.

JOHN ROSEMOND

Every family has its share of hassles and bores or, worse, those who make family get-togethers less than perfect. Children will learn how to deal with relatives who have flaws by observing their elders. Think of it as training for their future. Families are a slice of life. Learning how to get along in the family prepares children for coping with the other difficult people they may encounter, such as grumpy teachers, an egomaniacal boss, an alcoholic co-worker or an argumentative neighbor. Sometimes it is these difficult family members who surprise us with their support in times of need. They understand what it's like to have problems.

Grandparents set the tone for family interactions by the respect they show their adult children and by granting them autonomy. They need to be apart from, yet also a part of, the family. How to maintain separateness affectionately is a dilemma. When you intrude, even with the best of intentions, angry feelings erupt. Easier family relationships are based on a recognition that we are no longer in charge of them. When we let go and let them make their own mistakes, we are allowing them to learn by experience. After all, isn't that the way we learned?

Changing Family Interaction

When faced with family problems, you might consider questioning your usual responses. You can change problems that occur by changing the pattern of your interaction. Family therapist Dr. Constance Ahrons, author of *The Good Divorce,* suggests ways to change family patterns that perpetuate feuding. Family members can learn to disagree agreeably. We should fight the feud, not just each other, by keeping these thoughts in mind:

— Your goal is to break a pattern by understanding what's really going on between you and the other person, below the surface of the battle. This involves a commitment on your part to change the situation.

— In order to repair a relationship you must really care about how the other person feels, not just how you are hurting. It's no good to ask crucial questions if you don't really want to hear the answers.

— Stop fighting for your own point of view. Investigate instead how the two of you are participating together to create the problem.

Life must be understood back-ward. But it must be lived forward.

KIERKEGAARD

— Separate what you two can talk about from those things that are too hot to handle. Back off when the fight erupts, saying, "Let's discuss this later."

— Treat the other person respectfully. In feuds, each person feels disrespected by the other. People can fight hard, but if they respect each other, it never ends up as a feud—it ends up as a disagreement.

— Invite a third party to mediate. It can be a friend or relative you both respect, a member of the clergy or a family therapist. With a neutral third party present, people are less apt to explode and more tends to get resolved.

A Story of Mediation

Today mediation is being used successfully to settle family conflicts, resolving disputes quickly and economically. Family issues that arise from disagreements or divorce that often lead to permanent estrangement are being settled amicably. This story, told to me by a lawyer/mediator, demonstrates an effective family mediation.

The participants:

Ben, a ninety-year-old widower who recently underwent heart surgery.

Ida, his eighty-seven-year-old friend and lover.

Sharon, Ben's fifty-seven-year-old daughter who manages his business affairs and feels responsible for her father's welfare.

Tim, Ben's thirty-two-year-old grandson and Sharon's son.

The problem:

Ben asked Ida to take a drive with him in his car, despite doctor's orders that he should not drive. Ida agreed to go with him. Upon hearing of this, Sharon was convinced that Ida had exercised poor judgment and could not be trusted. Sharon felt that her father was in jeopardy and should be put in a home where he would be properly supervised. Ben did not want to change his present lifestyle. Tim was worried about his grandfather and concerned about his mother's stress.

The process:

According to the mediator, they entered the mediation room expressing doubts about the process. The mediator asked each participant to tell his story while the others listened without comment and facilitated the speaker by asking questions. As they listened to each other, the dynamics began to change, and things were seen in a whole new light. Ida's role was redefined as a girlfriend who was not inclined to tell Ben what to do, rather than a person with faulty judgment. Sharon understood and said, "Of course, if I told my husband what to do all the time he'd leave me."

The outcome:

Tim was in a pivotal position because he was seen as an ally by both his mother and grandfather. In this position, his was a voice of reason. Ben was able to maintain his independence and expressed gratitude for his grandson's support. Their special grandfather-grandson bond endures.

Sibling Rivalry Never Ends

Sibling rivalries never end. Love between family members is not automatic. Closeness causes strong emotions that can be loving or hateful. Sometimes grandparents inadvertently promote jealous feelings in their adult children or grandchildren. Jealousy is a natural emotion. In fact, you may find yourself

How do you get along? Can you let others do the talking even when you know more about the subject than they?

experiencing a bit of grandparent rivalry. For example, how did you feel upon hearing that the other grandparents were doing something wonderful with the kids, or that they've given the kids a fabulous gift, or that your children have decided to spend the holidays with them?

Of course, your reactions may not be totally logical or fair, but then that's what rivalry is—emotional and irrational. Recognizing those reactions in yourself will help keep you from acting on them. Keep your own counsel.

We never outgrow sibling rivalry. Grown children continue to be sensitive to favoritism. No matter how old we get, part of us remains the child in relationship to our parents. Our adult children may still be harboring perceived inequities from their own childhood and continue to compare how they and their siblings are treated. This requires awareness of their feelings in order to promote family harmony.

My grown daughter was hurt when I mentioned how well I thought my daughter-in-law was doing with her children.
GRANDMA DOT

Comparisons by parents stir competition. Children are all too aware of differences and don't need to be reminded. If one child is struggling to make it and another has hit it big, don't boast about it in their presence. It's a sure bet that will stir up bad feelings between them, and you will be the loser.

There are many inequities between family members. If you are able to spend more time with one set of grandchildren than another, be careful that you don't talk about it too much to the ones you see less often. It can easily hurt their feelings and stir up jealousy. You may not be able to change the situation; just try not to let it get in the way. Don't hold up one member of the family as an example for the others. This is guaranteed to create hard feelings. Even innocent comments can be taken the wrong way.

Sibling rivalries also extend into the next generation. Sharing parents or grandparents doesn't come naturally. As new grandchildren arrive, the older ones feel displaced. You can help to ease the adjustment to a new brother or sister by your reassurance that they are still special to you. And don't forget that there is such a thing as cousin rivalry. Relationships between cousins need the same kind of consideration.

When Grandma Lois arrived she hadn't given much thought to the gift she was carrying for the new baby. She was delivering it for a friend. When five-year-old Eva found that there was a gift for her baby sister and none for her, she ran upstairs crying. Grandma attempted to console her by describing how she had room in her heart to love each of her three children and now each grandchild. Eva was not convinced. Then Grandma said, "Well, Eva, just remember that I will always have loved you for five years longer than your sister!"

When there's a new baby, be considerate of the older grandchild's feelings by not carrying on over the new baby in front of her. Don't compare grandchildren to each other or to their parents. Remember that because you are important, your words pack an extra wallop. Saying things like, "Your sister is so good, and you were such a difficult baby," is guaranteed to hurt feelings.

Rivalries exist among cousins, too. "Why aren't you polite like your cousin?" or, "Your cousin gets better grades than you," will interfere with cousins forming close relationships. It's a blow to self-esteem and defeats your wish for a warm and close family.

Being aware of your own sense of rivalry with the other grandparents can help you to empathize with others. Don't talk against the other grandparents to your children or grandchildren.

Here They Come:
Visits to Grandparents

They're traveling *over the river and through the wood* to you! The anticipation is great. You can't wait. You plan and prepare. You end up needing a vacation. Here are some tips that prepare you for the reality and help you make the best of it. *Preparation* is the key to successful visits. Young children do best when their regular routine is not interrupted and they don't get over-stimulated or overtired. Don't impose your ideas on your visitors. Offer suggestions, but let them decide what they want to do. If you have tickets for an event, let them know in advance. It's something special for them to look forward to and will help them plan. Remain flexible and allow time for just hanging out. That is often the most enjoyable time and provides the best quality interaction. These tips will help you enjoy your family's visits.

Prepare Yourself:

— Remind yourself that family gatherings are going to be hectic and take a lot of energy; get ready by being rested when they arrive.

— Get ready to put your life on hold. Keep your own social plans to a minimum; cancel such events as your regular tennis game. Notify your friends that you're going to be busy.

— Tie up loose ends so you'll have as much free time as possible.

— If you work and can't take time off, try to arrange a lighter schedule.

— Prepare yourself for the inevitable letdown when they leave. Plan something you can look forward to, to ease your sense of loss when the house is suddenly quiet again.

Prepare Your House:

— Take a tour of your house from the point of view of the ages of your visitors to determine what needs to be put away.

— Childproof your house by putting away breakables. Even older children running through the house can bump into things, so put special things in safe places.

— Keep pills and poisons, including cleaning products, out of reach.

— Put safety covers on electrical outlets for babies and toddlers.

— Eliminate dangling electric cords.

— Use folding gates if necessary to define safe space and to protect from potential hazards such as stairs.

— Comb the house for small items that a child could swallow, such as coins or paper clips or toys with small pieces.

— Have first-aid materials and simple medications on hand, such as baby aspirin, band-aids, anti-bacterial salve, thermometer, anti-diarrhea preparations, ice packs.

— Help visitors feel as much at home as possible by finding out in advance what they need, such as crib, high chair, car seat, potty, a place for diaper changing, diapers, wipes. You can rent or borrow the furniture. Make certain that cribs, high chairs and car seats meet current safety standards.

— Have emergency numbers handy by the phone, such as for the doctor, the poison-control center, a neighbor.

— Obtain an emergency medical release form giving you authority to authorize treatment for a child if the parents can't be reached. (This is valuable whenever and wherever you may babysit.)

Grandma Redhair kept toys, books, crayons in a special cupboard within easy reach of the grandchildren. When they arrived they made a bee-line to that cupboard to discover what new toys might have been added. Her great-grandchildren are now repeating the same ritual.

— Do marketing in advance and have their favorite foods and snacks. Find out what their breakfast routine includes and about special dietary needs.

Prepare for Activities:

— Children do best when their schedules and routines remain as unchanged as possible.

— Inquire in advance what they might want to do. Don't assume you know.

— Plan activities for children with crayons, art projects, books and videos.

— Create a space where they can play and do projects.

— Develop your own permanent collection of toys, books, videos, art materials and games. Children will remember and look forward to them.

— Make sure children have an opportunity for physical activity to burn off energy.

— Build in some *alone time* for each adult away from the crowd.

— Don't overschedule by making too many plans that will wear everyone out and shorten their tempers.

— Remain flexible and ready to change plans, even if you're disappointed. When you are disappointed, don't let that spoil the visit.

— Don't promote rivalries by comparing; accept each member of the family for who she or he is.

— Use the visit to demonstrate and teach your culture and heritage.

— If the visit includes some special meals, attempt to prepare as much as you can in advance.

Roll with the Punches by Remembering:

Plans get changed (planes get canceled, roads get closed).
Kids get sick.
Your household will be disrupted, and so will you.
Your house will get messy.
Kids don't sit still through dinner.
Not to criticize your children's parenting.
Decide to have fun!

Grandma Betts and Grandpa Tom announced, "We're plum tuckered out and resting up after having our grandchildren visit. We had a wonderful week riding bicycles, snorkeling and hiking, but we are utterly exhausted. When they left we sat outside with a drink, just enjoying the peace and quiet, and just forgot about dinner. We're too old for this."

"The thing that makes me mad," Grandma Betts continued, "is that we just don't have the energy we used to. In my mind, I feel I should *Aging is when your mind makes promises your body can't keep.* have the energy I had at forty, but being with the kids reminds us that we're in our sixties. We really must stay in shape."

When the timing of family visits is inconvenient, those pictures of stereotypical grandmothers holding rolling pins and smiling sweetly from the magazines of our youth can make us feel like impostors—like the grandmother who confessed to me, "I need to find out if it's all right to tell my daughter that I don't miss my grandchildren, even though I haven't seen them for weeks. She needn't feel obligated to visit so regularly. Some weekends I prefer sitting quietly in front of my computer rather than in the midst of their noise."

Then there are the mixed feelings expressed by Grandma Shari about her husband's family. "I work, so my free time is really at a premium. Lee's kids are nice enough, but they're not like my own. I feel obligated to help out with the grandchildren, but my heart's not in it. I know they're disappointed that I'm not more involved. Lee has more time to see them than I do, and that's fine with me. Although no one talks about it, the situation is a bit strained."

Grandma Beth chimed in. "I'm a professional woman. I'll never make it as a 'real' grandmother—you know, like in a Norman Rockwell painting."

Many grandparents express the feeling that they're not doing enough for their grandchildren. As one grandmother confided, "It's really a priority in my life. I feel it's my responsibility, that they need me. But I need me, too, and so does my husband. This is our time while we're both still healthy to enjoy our lives together. I'm torn by the feeling I never do enough and end up permanently guilty."

Meals

The important daily ritual of the family meal has practically disappeared. It has been described as the most important hour in the day for the family. Hurried families seldom gather together at the end of the day to talk over the day's happenings. Mealtime, sitting together at a table and sharing food and ideas, is a valuable experience because it forms a family community. It is around the table that ideas, culture and values are exchanged. It is a time for the family to celebrate its own values.

The tales we cherish—as families, communities and nations—are tools for making sense of our journey. Packed into our tellingware are instructions for living life right and connecting with one another.

DAN YASHINSKY

It provides a sense of belonging. You can provide this rich experience for your grandchildren and your family by planning family meals that promote the exchange of ideas and fellowship. The food does not have to be elaborate but might include favorite dishes of the past that reflect your culture. It can be simple but significant.

Family meals offer unlimited opportunities for learning, for celebrating, and for reinforcing in your grandchildren the significant values and ideals that guide your life. Initiate a discussion by posing a question to get things going. For example: "How do you know the sun will rise tomorrow?" "What did you think of the president's speech?" "How much television viewing is okay?" Make this a family discussion on critical television viewing and developing media literacy. Then make sure that everyone gets a chance to talk. Holidays suggest questions by their very nature. For example, a Thanksgiving question might be: "What are you thankful for?" or, for the New Year: "What do you hope for in the coming year?" Prime the pump with relevant

By the time a child is eighteen, with average television viewing, he has seen two hundred thousand murders.

questions designed to draw people out. This teaches children how to express themselves. Storytelling is another way to make family dinners personal and memorable.

Nutritious Snacks

Today's parents often insist on providing only healthy snacks for children, leaving grandparents at a loss for what they can offer as a special treat. I'm pleased that my children are aware of what their kids eat and how important it is to their healthy functioning. There are too many "little dumplings" today as a result of sedentary and fast-food habits. Sometimes it is fun to splurge on a wonderful sugary treat, but it's safer to do it with the parents' permission.

You can set a good example with these ideas for good nutritional treats:

Egg cups in the shape of chickens and ducks delighted my kids, and now the same cups make soft-boiled eggs an event for my grandchildren and a nostalgic moment for their parents.

— FROZEN BANANAS. Put banana on a stick if desired. Dip in orange juice, roll in wheat germ and freeze.

— PEANUT BUTTER TREATS. Combine ½ cup peanut butter with ¼ cup nonfat milk powder, ⅓ cup rolled oats, and ½ teaspoon cinnamon. Two tablespoons honey may be added for sweetness. Shape into one-inch balls and chill. *(Very young children can have allergic reactions to peanut butter, so do not serve this to those under the age of seven.)*

— FRUIT-SICLES. Use fruit juice or fruit puree (fruit pureed in blender). Pour into small paper cups or popsicle molds. Insert sticks and freeze.

— YOGURT-SICLES. Whip 1 cup plain low-fat yogurt in blender with ½ cup chopped fruit. Follow above freezing instructions.

— APPLE FROSTED WITH CREAM CHEESE. Core apple, slice across and dip in orange juice to prevent browning. Spread cream cheese on apple slice and top with another slice.

— FROZEN GRAHAM SANDWICHES. Sandwich 2 tablespoons frozen yogurt (slightly softened) between two graham crackers. Freeze until firm.

— FRUIT "GELS." Combine 2 packages of plain, unflavored gelatin with 2 cups fruit juice. Heat and stir until gelatin is dissolved. Pour into pan and chill until set. Cut into shapes with cookie cutters.

— APPLES. Turn into an inviting snack by using special tools like an apple slicer that cores and cuts into a circle of slices all at once or an apple peeler that miraculously turns and pares the fruit. Add a little cheese or some raisins or sprinkle with cinnamon.

Sharing the Pleasures

Don't overlook the benefits of grandparenting together with other grandparents. There is a particular pleasure in sharing. Grandma Pauline provided a welcome break in my routine by inviting me to bring my granddaughters for a day at her lakeside cabin. I was babysitting for the week, and not only was my energy flagging, but I was also beginning to long for some adult conversation. This successful outing combined kids of varying ages. We fixed lunch together, picnicked and played in the water. It gave me an infusion of energy and extended the social experience of the kids with the inter-generational interchange that is so sorely needed today. Sharing our families also gifted me with a deepened bond of friendship.

When Grandma Phyllis's granddaughter Sarah visits, we get together with my grandson Harrison to promote their budding friendship. Who else but another grandparent would find their interaction so absolutely compelling? By participating together, we become interested in hearing each other's grandchildren stories. It extends the family.

When we visited our friend Sara in her cabin in the mountains, her two granddaughters and our granddaughter spread out the chores, made a variety of playmate combinations possible, and allowed the adults to have a little time for themselves. That joyous week included intergenerational swimming, cooking, hiking, horseback riding and square dancing. A week like that provides the glue that holds friendships fast.

DOs AND DON'Ts

1. DO realize that perfection is an unrealistic standard; all families have flaws.

2. DO learn to disagree agreeably.

3. DO consider a mediator when problems get out of hand.

4. DON'T compare children; it stirs up jealousy and threatens family solidarity.

5. DON'T forget that rivalries extend to cousins.

6. DO prepare for your family's visits.

7. DO build in some alone time for your visiting kids.

8. DO take care that mealtime provides opportunities for family discussion.

9. DO encourage a healthy lifestyle for grandchildren with nutritious snacks and exercise.

10. DO participate together with other grandparents and their grandchildren.

8

Grandfathers: Overcoming Gender Myths

Younger and middle-aged men need a relationship with an older man. They desire to be with an older man who talks. They need to be admired by an older man.
Iron John, ROBERT BLY

Overcoming Gender Myths

Grandfathers, you have a most important job to do. You are role models. Don't be discouraged by popular myths to the contrary. Grandfatherhood is a chance to make the difference only you can make. This is also your opportunity to re-experience the wonderment of childhood. It is your time to be teacher and leader, to explore another side of yourself, to take the time to talk to younger men and children. When your own kids were young, you probably didn't have the time to spend with them. Many grandfathers are now making up for the experiences they missed by their involvement with grandchildren, and fathers find that the encouragement of their seniors gives them an improved sense of maleness and a stronger sense of self.

Younger and middle-aged men need older men who admire them and whom they can admire.

> "In a completely rational society, the best of us would aspire to be teachers and the rest of us would have to settle for something less, because passing civilization along from one generation to the next ought to be the highest honor and the highest responsibility anyone could have."
>
> LEE IACOCCA

The whole of humanity is divided into two groups by virtue of their sex. Drs. Louise Ames, Frances Ilg and Sidney Baker point out that while many behaviors commonly associated with being male or female are, at least to some extent, a product of the culture, the earliness and persistence of many sex differences indicate that many traits do have a constitutional basis. Girls, for example, generally mature earlier than boys and are generally more interested in the person, in social relationships; boys are more interested in objective reality and how things work. These differences can easily be overstated; the lines of demarcation are not sharp, but our culture depends on the participation and input of both males and females, as do our families.

A hero is someone who has given his or her life to something bigger than oneself.
JOSEPH CAMPBELL

Why is it that I feel so competent at work and so inadequate at home?
Father of young children commenting on his wife's criticism

Girls and boys have different styles; when they become mothers and fathers they have very different styles of parenting, so it follows that grandmothers and grandfathers will have differences, too. What are those differences, and what are the myths that reinforce gender bias and inhibit full participation of both, which is so important to the child? Customarily, mothers assume the executive function over the children with the intimate, hands-on role. Fathers tend to feel clumsy in their parenting. Those mothers and grandmothers who don't accept the differences in styles or

As I watched my wife play on the floor with our grandbaby, I felt envious. I don't know how to play with a baby.
POP-POP EDDIE

experience discourage male participation by their criticism. Unfortunately, this may be encouraged by the many television fathers who are portrayed as bumbling, inept and out of touch with their hip children. Everyone misses out when the men are not actively involved.

Frank Lloyd Wright remembered walking with his grandfather in the snow, then running off and observing the path they had made. He called this kind of seemingly goalless time, "meandering."

How can fathers and grandfathers be encouraged to assume their essential role?

Myths

1. Child-rearing is women's work. They do it better.
2. Grandfathers are less interested in child development.

    Myths are so powerful that we internalize them even when they contradict our deepest experience.
    GLORIA STEINEM

3. Grandfathers don't know how to take care of children and are insecure in such a role.
4. Grandfathers are still working and are too busy for the children.
5. Grandfathers are less sensitive to change and the pace of young people.

These myths may be dispelled, first, by recognizing them and, then, by objecting to them in yourself; these are the initial steps to change. However, too often they linger, to give way only after great anxiety and painful experience, some- *I learned kindness from* times leading to alienation and dissension in *Grandpa Joe.* the family. Today's fathers may be assuming a STEVE, age thirty-three more hands-on parenting role, and grandfathers can follow their lead. Tragically, an increasing number of fathers and grandfathers are simply not there, and many who are there need encouragement to: surrender the stereotypes of maleness that inhibit them, show tenderness, share in the nurture of the young.

Just as it is important for children of all ages to experience both mothers and fathers, a child also needs both grandmothers and grandfathers. They need to experience grandfathers as caregivers. Grandfathers are role models for both their male and female children. As a grandfather, you influence attitudes and behavior. You are playmates and educators. Never underestimate your importance.

There are fathers who do not love their children; there is no grandfather who does not adore his grandson.

Victor Hugo

A moving testament to the influence of grandfathers was evident at the funeral of Israeli Prime Minister Yizhak Rabin when his eighteen-year-old granddaughter moved the world with her words, "Grandpa, you are my hero. I want you to know that." She said through her tears, "Everything I did, I always saw you before me."

Exchanging Roles

A grandchild thrives with two grandparents. How are their roles differentiated, and what surrogates or substitutes are to be found for a missing parent? Are there grandfathers for hire or exchange? Does the reversal of roles offer some positive benefits? Grandpa Bill and Grandma Joann evidently think so.

The torch has been passed.

Harold

Activist and proud grandfather, referring to his college-age granddaughter's newspaper article expressing the political point of view he has long championed.

"I'm more nurturing than Joann," Grampa Bill, a massive six-foot five-inch fellow, stated with pride. He explained that when his own children were growing up he was busy building his business and didn't have much time for them. Now in retirement, he's making up for lost time with his enthusiastic grandfathering of four-year-old Billy. He is cognizant of his importance as a role model, particularly because Billy's dad lives in another state. His delight over the fascination of viewing the world through this child's eyes is evident.

Every generation revolts against its fathers and makes friends with its grandfathers.

Lewis Mumford

Meanwhile, Grandma Joann is just as delighted to finally have time to pursue her work as an artist. "I've done that (raised children). Of course I love little Billy dearly, but it's true, I'm less involved with him than Bill."

Grandpa Bert agreed to take care of his six-year-old grand-daughter. She attends a year-round school and was off track and bored, so he took her for a week to the family's weekend retreat.

"It was just the two of us," he said, smiling. "We biked and gardened and just hung out together." Where was Grandma Ann? She was grappling with her duties as a commissioner on the Los Angeles Police Commission.

I need a place to complain about this huge family that's developing around me, whose web I have woven and in which I am now trapped, just at a time when I am experiencing the long-postponed desire to get in touch with my own spirit.

These grandmothers are pursuing new interests or careers while the grandfathers experience child-rearing. Both take advantage of the opportunities that accompany change to satisfy unmet needs. They are challenging the myths around expected roles. We can learn to value the differences that gender naturally offers while encouraging exchange of our traditional roles. Grandfathers will find sustenance in their relationships with grandchildren.

These reversals of stereotypical roles are not uncommon, but the benefits are often not appreciated. Many grandmothers are using their freedom from family responsibilities to follow interests they've put off or deferred. At the same time, grandfathers, by active involvement with their grandchildren, are enjoying experiences they missed as fathers. This crossover of roles takes advantage of opportunities that accompany change and becomes all the more crucial in the face of family dissolution, divorce, death or prolonged absence.

Grandchildren learn more from modeling than they do from advice.

We can learn to value the differences that gender naturally offers, to encourage crossover, to search for willing, designated surrogates, and to celebrate the feedback of a truly dynamic family loop.

Avoiding Stereotypes for Girls and Boys

This story, by Sunday school kindergarten teacher Mary Jane, is an example of how early sex roles were fixed in these five-year-olds. "I drew a large picture of the church that

> stretched across the front board and asked each of the twelve
> students (six girls, six boys) to draw themselves in the church.
> The boys drew themselves all over the place; several were on
> the pulpit, one was swinging from the chandelier, and one
> drew himself over the stained glass window of Jesus. The
> girls? They uniformly drew themselves sitting demurely in
> the pews, with one in the aisle."

Often without realizing it, we perpetuate stereotypical attitudes and behavior in children by our differing expectations and responses to girls and boys. We even speak differently to boys and girls from the time they are born. For example, fifteen-month-old Mandy is always addressed, "Oh, cutie," and, "Oh, sweetie." At the same age her brother had nicknames like "little man" or "pony boy." And although boys and girls do come with inherent differences, the expectations we set forth for them shape the expectations that children have for themselves. Being aware of this trap will help you avoid sending messages that may devalue your grandchildren or limit their choices in life.

Both girls and boys need praise and encouragement; the problem is that boys are more likely than girls to get it. In a study by the American Association of University Women, reported in *Short-Changing Girls, Short-Changing America,* a clear and often unconscious gender bias by school teachers was discovered. Teachers rewarded girls for being quiet and not interrupting while being more tolerant of disruptions by boys. They encouraged boys by calling upon them more often and did not expect girls to display high performance in science and math or sports. When this study was brought to the teachers' attention, they were shocked, for they had been completely unaware of their attitudes.

It is crucial that girls learn to become independent and self-sufficient. Most girls are unprepared for the life they will lead. Seventy-five percent of women work outside the home during their lifetime. Since being in the workforce is taken for granted for boys, they receive encouragement and training to develop their interests and skills. Girls are less likely to be encouraged to prepare for future work, unless it is some work to fall back on, with the expectation that they are expected to be dependent on a man. More attention is given to staying clean and looking pretty. It is evident from early childhood that both girls and boys are influenced by these gender stereotypes. They are most often perpetuated, without much awareness, by the family's expectations and attitudes by:

1. The expectations of the family: from the start, young children are in a search for gender identity, looking for clues about how they are expected to act.

2. The family's attitudes toward the children's interests and activities: by the time a child is four years old, she or he can pass a pretty sophisticated test on who grows up to have what jobs. It makes many adults uncomfortable when children ask for toys or express an interest in activities more traditional for the other sex, like trucks or balls for girls or dolls or cooking activities for boys.

> *I ask each grandchild, "Do you know what grandfathers are for? They're for talking to about the things you can't talk about with your parents." It works. Because of our heart-to-heart talks I've had the opportunity to give direction to some of their life decisions.*
> GRANDPA HERB

Tips for Overcoming Gender Stereotypes

Psychologists Toni Bernay and Dorothy Cantor interviewed female leaders who agreed that five "messages" they received during childhood gave them the strength and courage to develop their talents and to become women of leadership. Although both boys and girls need these messages to succeed, they are less likely to be given to girls than to boys. The messages are:

1. You are loved and special.

2. You can set goals and do anything you want, as in, "You can do the same things the guys do."

3. It is permissible to take risks.

4. You can use and enjoy "creative aggression, which allows you to set a goal and go after it and stand up for what you believe in."

5. You can dream of greatness.

Check your beliefs against these stereotypes and make a special effort to encourage your granddaughters, as well as your grandsons, to become self-sufficient and active participants in life. Once again, your male point of view can play a critical role in their development. On the other hand, boys are rarely encouraged to show their emotions, to be nurturing and caring, or to learn how to take care of themselves by learning to cook, do their washing or clean. They are not prepared for everyday self-sufficiency and are then uncomfortable with their fathering role. Girls are seldom encouraged to be active participants, to plan for interesting lives, to develop skills, or to think about the work in their future. By limiting our children, we're shortchanging them.

What Girls Need: What You Can Do

— Praise girls for their skills and successes, not just their appearance.

— Encourage girls to exert themselves physically, including getting dirty, disheveled and sweaty.

— Teach girls to critique media portrayals of women and girls in terms of what image they promote and why.

— Write letters of complaint to toy and publishing companies that promote sexist products.

— Make sure that youth activities offer girls opportunities for leadership.

— Debunk the myth that girls grow up to be taken care of by a man. Most women will work outside the home for much of their lives.

— Introduce girls to dynamic women who can take care of themselves, including those who combine paid work, volunteer work and family life.

— To be admired by grandfathers and grandmothers.

Reprinted from *Past the Pink and Blue Predicament: Freeing the Next Generation from Sex Stereotypes*. Published by Girls, Inc. National Resource Center.

What Boys Need: What You Can Do

We are accustomed to viewing the world with a male perspective, with the patriarchal bias of Western history. Boys inherit that view; and the culture of maleness perpetuates it, indeed, promotes it, in the image-making and advertising industries of entertainment, TV, film, clothing, sports and automobiles. Yet, this view is limiting to both sexes. Research and practice in the professions of childcare, parenting and mental health challenge that view and hold out the merit of—and the need for—transcending that bias in preparing children and adults for the best possible life. Become aware of your own preferences for certain traits, so there is less likelihood of your passing them on in a negative way.

To paraphrase Dr. T. Berry Brazelton: "Despite the desire of modern [grand]parents to treat children of either sex in the same way, the child of the opposite sex will have a particular appeal to each [grand]parent. You will inevitably treat children differently because of their sex. What you must not do is devalue either one. Just as every little girl needs an admiring [grand]father, every boy needs a [grand]mother who believes that 'he's the greatest boy of all.'"

The difficulty for the child arises when the parents are not comfortable with their sexual identities, when they feel inadequate as men or women.
ERNA FURMAN

— About 40% of the nation's children are not living with their fathers.

— Some 31% of all American babies are born out of wedlock, up from 5% in 1960.

> — More than half of all marriages end in divorce, and many kids suffer through more than one breakup.
>
> — It's not simply a matter of the additional money fathers bring to the household. Money influences what you have and what you can do. Fathers shape who you are.
>
> THE DENVER POST

Tenderness and a show of feelings by men and boys is now okay. Senators, candidates and even presidents may cry in public. Football players celebrate with hugs, and country western lyrics drip with emotion over patriotism and unrequited love. The realm of politics has been opened to women, and while gender bias is far from dead, the stereotypes of role in public service and public discourse are giving way. Inequities in behavior based on gender are increasingly recognized and uniformly criticized. No one wants to stereotype boys and girls.

Boys Need To:

— have role modeling by both sexes, acknowledging difference

— experience activities beyond stereotypes—washing dishes as well as washing cars

When asked what it was like to be a woman in Congress, Pat Schroeder responded, "I have a uterus, as well as a mind, and they both work."

— question the need to be macho by denying feelings and avoiding tears

— become aware of the inequities based on gender

— develop a consciousness of how society is generally seen from a male point of view—in the home, in the school, in the marketplace, in work and politics, in the management of money, in the experience and practice of sex

— have opportunities to learn self-sufficiency in such activities as cooking, doing the wash, setting the table (their wives will expect them to help)

— develop male competence, skill and self-esteem; achieve autonomy and confidence in decision making; exercise authority, discipline and rules; learn to respect limits

— accumulate work experiences—getting along with people, learning how it feels to be useful and be rewarded for it, receiving recognition and its rewards

— have opportunities to participate in the arts

— be admired by grandfathers

How clear it is that the example, the lived experience, of father and grandfather are powerful models for a boy's development—for help in meeting their needs and growing up a sensitive and healthy male. How vital is the responsibility to demonstrate the relationship of needs and values to the health of the family and the community, the search for social equality and justice. How great are the rewards for the grandfather who can show his grandchild "the road into the world."

My dad tends to be aloof, so he doesn't have much of a relationship with his six grandchildren. I am eager for my children to know their grandfather and make it a point to personally invite him to school, church and family functions. When invited he seems happy to attend. My brothers and sisters can't believe it and keep asking how is it that he is participating. It is really so easy. Evidently he just needs to be asked.

HILDA, mother of three

He likes to find some owls with me.
    He writes with me.
He sits next to me when I eat dinner.
    I like to sit next to him.
He shows me blue jays, the blue jays come down.
    We pick tangerines.
I love you, Grandpa.

NATHAN TO GRANDPA SAM,
Father's Day 1987

DOs AND DON'Ts

I learned about plants and farming from my grandfather. When I was a little boy in Guadalajara I carried a sack of seeds on my back and followed behind him in the fields. As he made the furrows in a straight line, he taught me to drop in the seeds to plant corn and beans. I marked off the distance between seeds with my feet and planted three or four corn and then some beans. The corn grew fast and supported the beans that wound around them as they grew. To this day, I thank my grandfather when I do my work.

RAMON GUERRERO,
Master gardener

1. DO let yourself be a hero.

2. DO be willing to challenge every myth and defy every stereotype.

3. DO pass the torch without letting go.

4. DO recognize that "just hanging out" is really something.

5. DON'T waste your maleness; somewhere a young man needs you.

6. DON'T forget that women can "hold up half the sky."

7. DO encourage girls who aspire to enter nontraditional careers, such as science, politics or the ministry.

8. DO encourage boys who aspire to enter nontraditional careers, such as elementary school teaching or nursing.

9

The Joys of Giving

Grandparents love to spoil their grandchildren.
ELOISE, age seven, when asked to describe grandparents

Gifts Have Power

Yes, by all means, give gifts to your grandchildren without worry that you're spoiling them. *Presents* is a grandparent's middle name. They help us express our desire for connection and our sheer delight in their existence. Every little treat or present says, "I think you're special," and deepens our ties.

Gifts are a reflection of our values and interests. They show our willingness to spend time, effort and money and are tangible evidence that we value them, while our choices demonstrate our understanding of their needs.

Gifts give us the power to influence, a chance to put in our two-cents worth. With our gifts we can introduce grandchildren to ideas and experiences. When you encourage learning and study with reference books, a study lamp, desk, computer or special classes, your gifts speak louder than words about the importance of education. Subsidizing interests and hobbies with classes, equipment and camps shows your interest in their experiences. But avoid precipitating a family crisis by getting the parents' permission first. Any gift that requires special attention or assembly, makes noise, needs supervision, will take up space or might be controversial for

159

any reason should be discussed with parents in advance before you mention it to the child. The parents will appreciate your consideration, and their input can help you avoid mistakes. Showing up with an unwelcome *surprise,* like a sugary treat or a live pet, could create a family crisis. Let good common sense prevail.

Try not to let your enthusiasm for a gift idea or an outing create tension between you, the parent and the child. Asking a child, *"How would you like a pony/a drum set/a trip to Disney World"* without clearance from parents can inadvertently cause trouble with a capital T.

I discovered this the hard way. It began innocently enough when I asked eight-year-old Eloise if she'd like to have her own tetherball after we enjoyed a game together at her school. It never occurred to me that I might be creating a problem. She was excited about having one of her own, but to our surprise, her parents nixed the idea because it would take up too much yard space. The last thing I wanted to do was to create a problem. Not only did I disappoint Eloise, I set parents and child against each other. I was frustrated to have my good idea squashed and disappointed by their reaction. At these moments I must take a deep breath and recall my grandparent mantra, "I am not in charge." I try to ask before I open my mouth, which is not always easy, and sometimes my enthusiasm gets the better of me. Fortunately my kids are good-natured and forgiving. I am learning to return the favor and allow them their choices.

Gifts Are Your Message

Viewing your gift as a vehicle that carries your message adds personal satisfaction. When looking for a gift, begin by choosing the messages you'd like to send. Would you like your gift to:

— introduce your grandchild to new ideas?

— stimulate imagination?

— encourage education?

— develop skills?

— provide new experiences?

— be a practical help?

— influence? How?

— encourage? What?

— support the family?

— be an answer to a prayer?

— offer pure delight?

— be just a little reminder that you're thinking of them?

— deepen your relationship?

Gifts, small or large, help you build relationships.

Review the life of the recipient for further suggestions. What are her interests? What is she into these days? What would *you like her to be thinking or doing?* This will begin to direct your thoughts. For more information, ask her or her parents. It's added insurance that your gift will be on target. Interests change. You may not realize that she's no longer into ballet and is passionate about soccer.

Thinking back to your own favorite childhood possessions and gifts, do any stand out in your memory? I remember the magazine subscription I received from my out-of-town Aunt Mimi and Uncle Earl every Christmas. I felt so grown-up having my own mail. The anticipation each copy brought is still a warm memory. That gift conveyed the message that I was special to them and that they knew what I would like. My first two-wheeler, the doll house with a swivel stand made by my father, a book explaining different religious beliefs entitled *One God: The Ways We Worship Him,* a large poster board with my name spelled out in crisp new dollar bills—all are treasured memories of the givers, as well. They are all gone now, but their thoughtfulness expressed in their gifts continues to connect us.

I also remember opening a present from my dear Aunt Rose. That nice white blouse just wasn't the *cool thing* to wear. I'm sure she spent a good deal of time and effort, and I really appreciated her thought, but it was a reminder of the distance between Ohio and California. She really didn't know me. It goes to show that the amount you spend doesn't necessarily determine success. That magazine subscription probably cost less than the blouse, was easier to buy and send, and didn't require a size.

My personal preference for giving a gift when it's needed, rather than waiting for a special occasion, has reaped rewards. Responding to a need with a gift when the desire and need are greatest sends the powerful message that you are a dependable supporter. A soccer ball is needed during soccer season, while the child is actively interested in playing and developing skills. Gifts should be timely; waiting for a birthday may be too late, a missed opportunity of need and connection.

> Nine-year-old granddaughter Caitie just asked for bongo drums for the band she and her friend want to start. She also expressed her interest in finding the music they'll perform. Well, that sounds good to me, especially since she just started violin lessons and this will further her interest in music. I want to support the positive interests of my children and grandchildren. She agreed to consider it a Hanukkah present, which is three months away. If I wait till then, her enthusiasm may have waned and a good experience missed. By showing my support at this moment in time, she knows I'm behind her; I'm her ally. Those bongo drums will send many messages: "I take you seriously. You have good ideas and I will support them. You can count on me." The drums become a vehicle to reaffirm our bond.

More Bang for Your Buck

Gifts don't have to be expensive to be wonderful. In fact, some of the things grandparents splurge on are a big waste of money. Save your money and forget those glitzy, colorful, plastic toys and the battery-operated gadgets. They miss the point of play and are quickly broken or discarded. Better to put the money in a bank account for the child. Today's children have too many toys. It confuses them. They are bored in the midst of plenty. Toys and play materials are much more than things to keep children busy or amused. Children use them for learning and to develop skills. They use them to express and cope with all kinds of feelings. They help children to:

We need to spend half as much money and twice as much time with our children.

> Transform feelings into action—
> Anger or high spirits get pounded into clay.
> The desire to be big and strong goes into building "the tallest building."
> A happy mood is enthusiastically painted in bright colors.

> Translate ideas into forms, concepts into shapes—
> A house of blocks, like a real house, has closed sides.
> A bridge is suspended above the ground.

> Translate impressions into products—
> A clay cookie is round and flat.
> A crayoned person has eyes and ears.

Children will take any material, shape or form and breathe a bit of themselves into it. The more flexible or unstructured the material is and the better it serves as an object on which they can project feelings and ideas, the more lasting it will be.

My mother-in-law established a relationship with a knowledgeable toy salesperson who helped her for many years to choose really fine, classic, age-appropriate toys. They were always such a big hit and provided so many happy hours of play that I've saved them for my grandchildren.
GRANDMA ELLEN

Play Is Serious

Play is more than the work of childhood. Play is an intrinsic part of a child's life. Through play, children express their feelings and integrate real and imaginary experiences. Through play, they try on future roles, such as mommy and daddy and fire-fighter. Through play, they learn about their bodies and how they work. Through play, they discover themselves and their world. Toys should help them explore and allow them to develop their imagination.

How a child plays out her feelings after getting a shot from the doctor is an example of play serving a child's emotional development. After receiving a shot from the doctor she will begin to play doctor, giving shots to dolls or playmates. This is a healthy response to her experience of being overpowered and hurt. Being in charge of giving shots is an attempt to overcome the frustration of being a passive victim at the mercy of the doctor. The child gains a sense of mastery, and equilibrium is restored.

Children act out their experiences in order to relieve their feelings of helplessness and gain control over them. They learn about the world around them by conducting scientific experiments—discovering how water pours, how mixing paint changes colors, or how a tower of blocks is balanced and then tumbled. They climb and run and hop and jump and find out what they can do. Attempts to direct their play may intrude on their feelings and violate their freedom. Though well-meaning, the adult who suggests, "Why don't you do it this way?" should do so thoughtfully, taking care that they are not undermining a child's creativity and self-esteem. Guide them to discover for themselves. Learning takes place through active participation, not passive observation.

Elaborate toys tend to intrude on a child's play by limiting initiative and imagination. Watching a mechanical monkey dance around is amusing for the first few minutes, but you really can't interact with it. What can you do with it? When a toy doesn't stimulate imagination, children quickly lose interest. A simple toy, one that can be used in many ways, is a long-lasting toy if it encourages all kinds of interaction. Blocks are a good example. Blocks can become so many things—a fort, a freeway, a house, a tool—it's all up to a child's imagination. Blocks also teach basic mathematical and scientific principles, such as proportional relationships and laws of gravity and stability. Of course, during block play children don't recognize that they are studying such serious subjects. By observing how engrossed a child can become in play, you can measure its value. A good set of hardwood blocks is a great investment and a present to which you can add. Lincoln logs, Legos, erector sets and art supplies are all good staples for creative play.

A word of caution about shopping for girls only in the *pink and purple* aisles and boys only in the sports and action hero sections: break out of the stereotypes. Girls love to build and play with trains and dump trucks, and they should be encouraged to do so. Boys enjoy being caretakers with dolls and cuddly stuffed toys, and they love cooking and crafts.

Do Your Own Public Relations

My gift-giving strategy for identifying me with my gifts is to choose a theme for my gift with the intention of adding to it later. Many toys or categories of gifts fit this model. Lego building sets, for example, or Brio trains, are long-lasting toys that hold a child's interest for many years. Right now I'm on the lookout for rhythm instruments for my three-year-old grandchildren Raeann and Harrison. Then I'll add music cassettes so they can play along.

My grandmother did a brilliant thing. For each birthday she gave me an antique painting or a drawing of a girl. This collection is a lasting legacy I continue to cherish as an adult.

You can also give gifts around a theme—a child's interest or hobby or something you wish to introduce. This is how our gifts have power. Let's say your grandchild has an interest in Native American culture. You might give books, articles of clothing, art work, music, videos, craft projects and, perhaps, a trip to an historic site—all pertaining to this topic. This not only connects you but gives you a common interest to pursue. Any topic of interest to you, such as American history, scientific inquiry, photography, the out-of-doors, or the environment, becomes a vehicle for expanding your grandchild's horizons and making a difference. Let your imagination be your guide.

A word of caution: beware of the high price of guilt and competition. Feeling guilty because you haven't spent enough time with your grandchild? Don't let that lead you into extravagant or foolish choices. Question your motivation and avoid the feelings of grandparent rivalry that push you to choose a gift for the purpose of making a big splash. Stirring up the jealousy of the other grandparents just perpetuates the "I'm a better grandparent than you" game. Your importance isn't measured by what you spend. A gift that's calculated to outdo others may not connect to the child at all. That four-foot stuffed bunny may eclipse an Easter basket, but it may also scare a little kid to death.

Five-year-old Caitlin took being in Big School very seriously and wanted a desk on which to do her homework. Giving her that desk has made me part of her new thrill of feeling grown-up and of learning. I feel I'm right there encouraging her while she sits at her desk practicing her letters.

More Gifts

Some kids love clothes, but most—particularly teenagers—have definite preferences. Some styles are *cool* and some are not. Again, when in doubt, ask. Clothes for young children should be practical. I watched a father struggle to put a wide, fashionable belt on his two-year-old daughter for several frustrating minutes. Why? Clothes can be fun, but they should be easy to wear and easy to take off for toileting. Have you ever watched a four-year-old struggle to get out of a jumpsuit in a hurry? Wearing hard-to-remove clothing makes a child worry about having an accident and doesn't foster independence. A family's lifestyle is another consideration when choosing a gift. A busy parent won't appreciate clothes that require ironing or cleaning.

Traditional children's clothing in China is made with a flapped rear opening permitting children to easily manage their own toileting.

Little gifts for no particular reason are special surprises. Stickers, materials to make valentines, a pair of colorful socks, a headband, some baseball cards, a seashell, a cartoon or article from the newspaper, cookies, a postcard or other things you will think of keep reminding them that they've got a grandparent who thinks of them.

Money is always welcome. It's empowering. It gives the recipient the freedom to make a choice of her very own, and it builds self-confidence. Even when the gift money is spent unwisely, it affords a valuable lesson in learning how to spend.

Money—it doesn't have to be large sums—deposited in a special bank account or invested teaches the value of saving. Investing money in a stock introduces the world of finance—especially buying a stock in a company the child can relate to, such as Ben and Jerry's Ice Cream, Mattel Toys, Disney or The Learning Company. Sometimes helping to secure the future costs no more than toys.

The gift of recycled clothing may connect family members in unexpected ways. Grandpa Sam still has pleasant memories of the durable and elegant white linen knickers handed down from older cousin Hugh. Worn for years, they carried the message of quality goods connecting cousins.

Generating new experiences and wider interests adds power to your input and makes a difference. Whether you encourage hobbies, music lessons, Little League or summer camp, your message is clear. You can take the initiative by suggesting an activity you are willing to support. Maybe it's an activity you enjoyed yourself or one you've always wished you had experienced. Tickets to a theatrical or sporting event are exciting and even more fun when you go along. Trips and outings have the added advantage of having the children to yourself. Children are quite different when they're away from their

Because of the regular deposits Grandpa Sam has made in a special account for his grandson, Nathan will soon be able to realize his dream, a horse of his own!

parents, usually much better behaved and more responsive to you. While sending the message, "You have grandparents who love you and care about you," you can introduce them to life's adventures.

While Papa and I were touring Wind Cave National Park with two granddaughters, Caitie and Morandi, the woman behind us began telling me that she had just finished a trip with her grandchildren.

"How was it?" I asked.

"Oh, it was great to have them away from their parents. Their mother, my daughter, is such a strict disciplinarian, it's hard to be around. I don't know where she got that. Not from me. I'm a teacher and would never be that harsh."

Your gift can also teach the value of giving to others. The object lesson that grandfather Jeremiah Kaplan devised for his grandchildren is an inspiring example of guiding the next generation by creatively using the power of gifts. He gave each grandchild over the age of eight $100 at Hannukah with the proviso that they give it all away by Passover. At that time he expected them to tell how and why they made their choices. There were no rules on how to do it. They could give it all in one chunk or spread it out in a hundred places. What Grandpa Jerry did was to create a situation which caused these children to think about giving and about the needs of others. They also had to question their responsibility to others and their power to effect change. Not everyone can afford to give their grandchild $100 for this purpose, but it certainly could be an effective lesson using a lesser amount.

When I was eight years old my grandfather taught me to read the stock market. At seventeen, I inherited $5,000 from him. It gave me my own credit and possibilities. I'm doing that for my children and grandchildren.

GRANDMA SARA JANE

Grandma Grace and Grandpa Harold are grandparents dedicated to social responsibility. By creating a family foundation for the purpose of bestowing small grants to causes of their choice, they have created a family forum for philosophic discussion on giving, combined with teaching how to make choices. The entire family—children and grandchildren over the age of ten—meet to deliberate. There are advantages beyond the stated goals of the foundation. Not only does it ensure that the whole family will gather together regularly (they all live in different cities), it becomes a communal exploration of values on many levels.

An indelible impression is made on grandchildren when we demonstrate our own values toward giving. That *tzedakah puske*, a blue box my grandmother kept on her kitchen sill, did more than plant trees in Israel. It informed me of her sense of responsibility. Attitudes are apparent in deeds. By giving a child a coin to drop in a box by the checkout stand or by supporting her school's fundraising project, we become examples of what we believe. That is our essential nature.

Donny and Gammy have asked that all of their children's gift giving to them be in the form of donations to a specific charity.

No, Thank You

It's a common complaint. You send a gift to your grandchild and eagerly wait for a response. Did she receive it? Did she like it? But you don't hear a thing. You have no idea if it was received and no clue to her reaction. The whole idea of sending the gift was to deepen your connection by letting her know that you remember her birthday. Without a response, you're left hanging in air. What should you do? Some grandparents get so angry and disgusted that after a while they decide to stop sending presents. Before you get to that point, consider these options.

First, ask the parents if the gift has been received, and ask them to ask your grandchild to acknowledge your gift with a note or phone call. Some parents just don't seem to understand the importance of a response or they put it off or are too stressed out to notice. They simply don't train their children in the important social graces and are doing their children a great disservice. It's a real turn-off, and others won't be as tolerant as grandparents.

Next, don't sit and stew; educate your grandchildren. Explain the importance of an acknowledgment, and explain why you want to hear from them. Let them know your present is sent to please them and to let them know they are in your thoughts, so you really need a response.

Then, enclose a stamped, self-addressed postcard. You can even demonstrate what is expected in a thank-you note by providing a place to check off: "Yes, I received your gift of the book, *Charlotte's Web*," and a partial

If you see a book, a rocking chair and a grandchild in the same room, don't pass up a chance to read aloud. Instill in your grandchildren a love of reading. It's one of the greatest gifts you can give.

BARBARA BUSH

sentence like, "I think it's _____," for them to fill in. If they're too young to write, ask them to draw a picture. By the way, this card can be enclosed even when the gift is delivered in person.

Keep communicating. Don't stand on ceremony, waiting for them to take the initiative. When approached without anger or criticism, instructing your grandchild in manners is a good deed. To make certain a package is received, send it so that it can be traced. I mailed a box of assembled goodies, including a photo album I'd spent a good deal of time on, to my granddaughters. It never arrived and was not traceable. I'm sadder but wiser now.

Your Guide to Great Gifts

Use this guide to stimulate your own ideas. Common sense tells you that because a gift is listed for a particular age group doesn't necessarily make it inappropriate for another age. Some things make great gifts for almost any age grandchild.

The one thing we never give enough of is love.
HENRY MILLER

GIFTS FOR ANY AGE

Tickets to theater, musical or sporting events and special events

Money: cash, stocks, bonds, investments

Lessons: sports, art, dance, music

Musical instruments

Art supplies

Hair cut or special grooming treatments

Transportation: plane, train, bus to visit you

Trips and vacations, with and without you

Magazine subscriptions: *Smithsonian, National Geographic, Highlights for Children, Sports Illustrated for Kids, National Geographic for Children*

Objects of art: poster art, prints, drawings and paintings

Camp

Extracurricular activities, such as Little League, scouting, Camp Fire

Calendars

Tutor

School tuition, from preschool onward

Medical: orthodontia, eyeglasses, surgeries, counseling; Testing for reading deficits, dyslexia, Attention Deficit Disorder or vocational aptitudes

Bedding: down comforters (which last for years) and sheets (especially flannel)

Books, books, books—all kinds—including books for entire family, e.g., art books, atlas, encyclopedia

Videos, especially on nature, history, classic stories

Cassettes, CDs, cassette or CD player

Radio

Clock

Framed photos of Grandma and Grandpa and the family

Computer and software

A note about choosing computer software: before you buy, see a demo to make sure it's what you like. Talk to the parents about their preferences. Some programs are frightening or violent and not appropriate for young children. Reading reviews will give you additional information.

BIRTH TO EIGHTEEN MONTHS

Cassette player

Cassettes: music and stories

Basket of books

Mobile, soft, cuddly toys (the lucky one will become a favorite companion)

Lambskin woolly

Soft ball

Spinning top

Playyard or playpen

Unbreakable crib mirror

Car seat

Baby carrier

Recliner seat

Stroller

High chair

Wipe-off bib

Training cup

Large Legos

Jack-in-the-box

Unbreakable dishes

Fork and spoon

Rocker for Mom and Dad

Digital thermometer

Illuminated ear-scope

Wagon with push bar

EIGHTEEN MONTHS TO THREE YEARS

Table and chair

Rocking chair

Teeter-totter

Sand toys: pail, shovel, sieve

Sandbox

Jumbo crayons

Dolls

Play-Doh

Dollhouse and sturdy furniture

Dollhouse family

Stuffed animals

Simple puzzles

Blocks

Large hollow blocks

Hammer and pegs

Push and pull toys

Broomstick horse

Rhythm instruments: sticks, triangle, drum

Pinwheel

Swing

Climbing equipment

Brio toys

Swimming pool

Water play toys

Electric toothbrush

Toy phone

Toy camera

Bathtub spout safety cover

THREE TO SIX YEARS

Step stool to reach the sink

Playhouse

Nesting boxes

Junk jewelry for dress-up

Dress-up clothes

Hats: fireman, cowboy, fancy

Tap shoes

Flashlight

Garden tools, seeds and bulbs

Wheelbarrow

Easel

Poster paints

Paper for drawing and painting

Art supplies: large crayons, markers, collage kit

Finger paints

Make-a-Plate

Scissors with blunt ends

Paper punch

Play kitchen

Tool bench

Cars and trucks

Wheel toys

Legos, fit-together construction toys

Lego table

Lincoln logs

Brio trains

Doctor kit

Autoharp

Toy phone

Tricycle

Ant farm

Birdfeeder

Stringing beads

Board games: Candyland, Picture Lotto, Hi Ho Cherrio

Bubble blowing liquid and wands

Hand puppets

Slide magnets

Sculpey nontoxic clay

CD-ROMs:

   How Many Bugs in a Box?, Simon and Schuster

   Math Workshop, Broderbund

SIX TO NINE YEARS

Backpack

Kites

Butterfly net

Jump rope

Recorder

Two-wheeler

Bicycle safety helmet

Lunch pail

Thermos

Board games: Monopoly, Parcheesi

Skates

Roller blades and safety equipment

Yo-Yo

Cards

Gyroscope

Picture dictionary

Puzzles: USA and world

Walkie-talkie

Watch

Dolls

Flower press

Computer

Computer software

Miniature dollhouse and furniture

Camera

Craft projects

Potholder weaving set

Art supplies: pastels, colored pencils

School supplies

Desk

Desk lamp

Desk chair

Sturdy outdoor clothes

Marbles

Magnifying glass

Basketball hoop and ball

Ink stamps and ink pad

Stable and horses

CD-ROMs:

> *My First Incredible, Amazing Dictionary,* Dorling Kindersley Multimedia
>
> *Scholastic's The Magic School Bus Explores the Solar System,* Scholastic
>
> *Peter and the Wolf,* TimeWarner Interactive

NINE TO TWELVE YEARS

Board games: Scrabble, RummiKube

Sleeping bag

Binoculars

Mountain bicycle

Bicycle helmet

Basketball hoop and ball

Computer

Computer software

Microscope

Camera

Calculator

Diary with lock

Backpack

Coin collection

Stamp collection

Cards for collecting: baseball, football

Duffel bag

Bulletin board

Pop-up tent

Tetherball

Marionettes

Pedometer

Sewing machine

Jigsaw puzzles

Playing cards

Magic tricks

CD-ROMs:

Encarta, Microsoft

The Way Things Work, Dorling Kindersley Multimedia

GeoSafari, Educational Insights Interactive

NFL Math, Sanctuary Woods

Where in the World Is Carmen Sandiego?, Broderbund

TEENAGERS

Portable cassette or CD player

Music cassettes or CDs

Sound equipment and speakers

Art supplies

Paints: oils, pastels, charcoal, watercolors

Pottery wheel

Building tools

Furniture and bedding for decorating their room

Luggage

Sports bag

Jewelry, special keepsakes

Wallet

Key ring

Watch

Telephone

Telephone answering machine

Book for journal-keeping

Computer and software

Sports equipment

Exercise equipment

Swiss Army knife

Hobby supplies

Photo albums

Scrapbook

Bead-stringing supplies

Tape deck

CD player

Clothes (risky; ask first)

Vocational guidance counseling

Pass to local movie theater

Money, money, money

Final Gifts

It is possible to undermine all of our efforts to build and main-tain family unity and solidarity with the inheritance we leave behind. No grandparent wants to leave a legacy of ill will, hard feelings and broken hearts over the transfer of family assets. The way your gifts are left can permanently rupture family relation-ships. You may say, "I don't have to worry, my kids wouldn't fight about money. They really love each other." Don't be too certain.

"I'm the one who worked hard, did well in school and became an engineer, and now I'm being punished for my success," my patient complained after learning that his portion of his parent's estate was less than his brother's. It was a serious blow and con-tinues to cause pain and create animosity between the brothers. You see, inheritance isn't just about money and possessions. What you leave and the way you leave it is a symbolic measure of your love and care. This applies to grandchildren, too.

Give yourself time to think about this issue before you make your will. Do you leave money equally, the same amount to each child, or will you divide it according to need? Your decisions rest upon philosophy, ethics and highly personal values. The questions and issues around inheritance, the gift giving sanctioned by the law, are many and I've illuminated them here for your consideration. The overarching questions have to do with what you want your money to say or achieve. How much control do you want or feel you need to have over the money? Do you want to give money and possessions before you die? Reflect on these complex questions.

— Should you talk it over with family before making inheritance decisions, or does that open a hornet's nest of competitive desires and speculation among spouse, children and grandchildren? I agree with Gerald and Jeffrey Condon, father-and-son estate lawyers, who point out in their book *Beyond the Grave: The Right Way and the Wrong Way of Leaving Money to Your Children* (and others) that in their vast experience, talking it over with the family is the best policy.

— Should you focus on giving to family or to dearly loved causes to which you may have given energy and resources?

— Are equality and fairness synonymous? How does need enter into your judgments?

— Do you want to exercise control to ensure your intended results, for example, to make sure your grandchild uses your money for education? Can you prevent squander and spousal abuse?

— How far down the generational ladder should you go? Spouse, children, grandchildren, great-grandchildren?

— How do you value the autonomy and trust the judgment of spouse and children?

— What is the consequence of your decisions on family feelings, community perceptions and your place in the public sun?

— Should your possessions be allocated to specific persons? Should you do this personally or wait until you are gone?

I have observed how inheritance can express the giver's wishes and values. A very wise man who had amassed a fortune exercised control beyond his time and ensured that his heirs would enjoy the fruits of his labor for generations to come. His heirs receive income only from his fortune and have no voice in money management. This has preserved the capital and protected his now-deceased daughter, who had a serious problem with alcohol and surely would not have been able to manage an inheritance that now provides a beautiful life for his grandchildren and great-grandchildren.

Don't scrimp in order to leave money for your children.
H. JACKSON BROWN JR.

My friend Betty expresses her values loud and clear to her grandchildren. She makes money available to them during her lifetime specifically for education or health needs.

Giving a grandchild a gift of a personal possession is a treasured connection. Specifying particular items in a will accomplishes that, too. I received a gold link bracelet from my grandmother's estate. It's a simple gift but a strong reminder of our connection and gives me particular pleasure with each wearing.

If I don't help my grandchildren while I'm alive, help may never come.
GERALD AND
JEFFREY CONDON

There are so many issues to consider, and each has ramifications for your family relationships and way of life. Considering them can ensure that your final gifts will bear the message you intend.

I like my children, but I really love my grandchildren.

DOs AND DON'Ts

1. DON'T overwhelm a child with too many gifts at one time.

2. DO buy good basic toys that encourage a child's imagination.

3. DO tell them why you chose a particular gift.

4. DO keep their lifestyle in mind and avoid making extra work for parents.

5. DO indulge in an extravagance if it's something she really longs for.

6. DON'T compete with others to give the biggest gift, especially other grandparents.

7. DO think about your grandchild's experiences and how you want to make a difference. Then do it.

8. DO send things that can stimulate their interests.

9. DO provide new experiences.

10. DO keep safety in mind. Anything that can fit through a toilet paper tube is something a small child can swallow.

11. DO check with parents before giving a gift that will require special care or arrangements, e.g., pets, overnights, travel.

12. DO send lots of little reminders, stickers, news clippings, photos.

13. DO give a child time to open and investigate a gift. Don't rush in with oohs and aahs.

14. DO consider the impact of inheritance on family feelings and solidarity.

15. DON'T wait for a will to distribute your personal possessions.

16. DON'T let the courts plan your estate.

17. DO give generously of the greatest gift of all, YOU.

10

The Essential Grandparent Reading Circle

Time—The Best Things in Life Are Free

Your time is the greatest gift of all. Sharing yourself—your ideas, the world, your passions, your history, and listening are priceless. In this hurry-up world, unhurried time is a demonstration that there is another way. Reading, teaching skills, working or playing together, or just "hanging out" is giving of yourself. Gifts you make—knitting a sweater or baking cookies or building a shelf or writing a letter—all send your personal message of caring. I told Caitie that when she wears the sweater I knit for her, to think of it as a hug from her Grandma Lilly that keeps her warm.

We show our interest and approval with the time we take to attend the grandchildren's sporting events and recitals. Even when our

My grandparents taught me to love nature and the out-of-doors.

DAVID, eighteen years old

When my granddaughter was visiting, we went to the knit shop so that she could be measured. She designed the sweater she wanted and lined up all the possible yarns to make her choice. I've never made a sweater as quickly.

schedules make it difficult, it's worth making it a priority. The best and most obvious benefit derived by giving of ourselves is that we get back so much more than we give.

> There has been much written about the decline of the traditional family and the increase in single-parent households. These trends have generated many new problems. However, volunteers can help fill the void by being "grandparents" to children without traditional families.
>
> As a surrogate grandparent, you can't take the place of parents, but being the best grandparent you can be is more important now than ever and can create that special bond that exists between grandparent and grandchild.

The Essential Grandparent Reading Circle: Helping the Children You Love, Love Books.

If you read to a child twenty minutes a day that child will learn 1 million additional words a year and will gain one thousand additional vocabulary words a year.

Delaine Easton
California State Superintendent of Schools

Reading aloud is a precious gift of time to your grandchildren that gives back to you in return. Not only is it a means for inspiring, nurturing and educating youngsters, but is it also a relaxing and enjoyable activity for grandparents. Time spent reading together helps form lasting bonds and creates fond memories for children to carry into adulthood.

Joining a community of readers will help keep alive your commitment to this heritage of lifelong learning, as well as keep you in touch with what's new in the world of books. Many libraries and bookstores with children's sections offer storytimes, where you and your grandchildren can listen and learn with others. Indeed, it is a wonderful way to connect with others who share a love of books.

If you see a book, a rocking chair and a grandchild in the same room, don't pass up a chance to read aloud. Instill in your grandchild a love of reading. It's one of the greatest gifts you can give.

Barbara Bush

To help in this effort, I have created The

Essential Grandparent Reading Circle. The Reading Circle is a guide for giving: giving *of* yourself and giving *to* yourself. It is a community of readers dedicated to inspiring children by reading to them. Research has shown that reading aloud to a child is the single most important factor in raising a child who loves to read. And reading is basic to learning.

If you have ever asked yourself "What can I do that really matters?" The Essential Grandparent Reading Circle provides an easy, doable answer. The new millennium beckons us to renew our commitment to our beliefs and values. We *Success is learned . . .* have an opportunity to shape the future by nurturing the younger generation. That includes all children, not only our own grandchildren. We are their role models and in them we find hope: the hope that provides the courage to live each day with energy and vigor.

We will share stories, new ideas and inspiration, have author interviews, update the research and find out what's new in books. Your participation will help to make this a *real* community. I look forward to welcoming you and receiving your suggestions.

By joining the Reading Circle you will be linking arms with others around the country who, like yourself, want to make a difference by reading to children. Do participate in our continuing dialogue via the newsletter by joining this community of readers. There is absolutely no charge or obligation and it is guaranteed to inspire your experience of reading to children. Just clip out the form in the back of the book on page 227 (or send your own). Print your name, mailing address and the age of the child or children to whom you'll be reading, add postage and mail it to me. Help the children you love, love books!

Dr. Lillian Carson's Essential Grandparent Reading Circle
1187 Coast Village Road, Suite 1-316
Montecito, California 93108-1725
Fax (805) 565-1049 or email *drlcarson@aol.com*
Web site: *www.essentialgrandparent.com*

The Essential Grandparent Reading Circle newsletter will keep you informed with reports on *why* reading to children expands their learning capacity and deepens relationships. It will offer tips for *how* to making reading to children a most rewarding experience and you will find guidance for *what* to read.

Why Read to Children?

Reading to a child would be rewarding enough if it was merely pleasurable and an opportunity for shared time, but it is much more. Science now demonstrates just how reading to children stimulates their brain development. Dr. Harry Chugani of Wayne State University has developed the technology to actually watch regions of a baby's brain become active while they listen. This activity expands the brain's capacity. We always knew that there was a correlation between being read to and the ability to read and now this technology offers scientific proof that reading to a child does make them smarter. And it's so incredibly easy to give this life-changing gift!

When reading aloud you are introducing sounds, words and ideas. You are stimulating curiosity and thought. It is education for a lifelong advantage.

Because children listen at a much higher level than they can read, many books such as *Little House on the Prairie, Charlotte's Web* or *Hans Christian Anderson's Fairy Tales* provide good listening for children who could not possibly read them themselves. They will understand and enjoy the story and extend their vocabulary at the same time. Listening also encourages children to concentrate, lengthening their attention span. The more often a child hears stories read aloud, the longer he or she will sit still and listen.

Promoting literacy, the Clinton Administration has allocated $128 million for programs to teach children to read. "Reading is the foundation for learning. The screen might as well be dark if a child is not able to read."

VICE PRESIDENT AL GORE

The literacy rate is one of the most widely used scales in the world for determining social and cultural development.

Educational inferiority is one of the greatest handicaps of all. According to the National Assessment of Educational Progress, only 60 percent of fourth graders read at a basic level or higher. Children who do not learn to read are destined for lives of insecurity and instability.

A volunteer reader in his children's classrooms, David was asked to read to yet another class. Being a busy man, his first inclination was to decline, but something prodded him to agree. In the new classroom he found a sense of freedom that allowed him to abandon inhibitions and have the fun of "hamming it up" with great expression and dramatic punch. He has now become an official reader for the school, sought after in many classrooms. He's discovered a new avenue for self-expression and is building a strong connection to the school, making his own kids so very proud.

A valuable by-product of reading to a child is the time spent together, truly a gift of oneself. Sharing the intimacy of reading and capturing a child's natural curiosity is an antidote to the hurried world. And you don't have to wonder if you are making a difference!

How to Read to Children

Reading is a perfect relationship builder. Make it special, when you can, by creating a cozy setting with a cup of tea and some hot chocolate in a comfy spot. But you don't have to wait for the perfect moment. You might just corral a kid and calm him down with a quiet and focused moment.

Research has shown that the average parent spends twelve and a half minutes a day with their child and the average kid sits passively in front of the television between four to five hours daily. These children hunger for human contact and input. They need the attention and comfort of a caring adult.

Many parents and grandparents are surprised by my answer to the often-asked question, "When should I begin to read to my child/grandchild?" The answer is: "now"; begin at birth, you cannot start too young. That's why books make such a good baby gift.

Infants are soothed by the sound of a voice, especially when it becomes familiar, and this answer is reinforced by the scientific research on brain development. Begin by showing the pictures and by introducing the objects in the book. By twelve months you can even teach a child to help turn the pages. For young children, just talk about the pictures without lingering too long on a page. Use the book however it feels right to you. Remember, you don't have to teach the ABC's with that lovely alphabet book to a one-year-old; just talk about the pictures. Reading to a child is interactive and requires the reader to respond to the child's attention span and interest. A child who grows up listening to books accepts reading as a part of life.

When reading, follow the child's lead. Don't hesitate abandoning a book when there is no interest. Children are entitled to their preferences, just as we are. Try to avoid reading when you are too tired or distracted. Kids recognize a half-hearted effort. It's also perfectly alright to express your disinterest in a particular book and move on to the next one. We're human, too. And remember, it's not necessary to read every word. Especially when reading to young children, learn to go with the flow of their interest. You might just point to the pictures, skip some pages and describe the story or forget about it as their interest dictates. Sometimes children just want to talk about what they see in the pictures. Older children, as well, may want to use this intimate time to talk about other things. Let go of your expectations and view reading as a vehicle for communicating thoughts and ideas and deepening relationships.

"You're never too old, too wacky or wild / To pick up a book and read to a child."

Reading to children is a perfect activity for those who want to nurture the young as a grandparent, parent, friend or mentor.

There are few activities that are so easy to perform and have such a big payoff.

Tips for Reading to Children:

- Create a cozy setting.

- Choose reading material that expresses thoughts and ideas you'd like to convey.

- Seek books that will deal with a child's immediate life issues such as potty training, sibling rivalry, starting school, divorce, or loss.

- Read above a child's ability to read on their own.

- Have fun by reading with feeling. Most adults feel less inhibited when reading to children because they don't feel they are being judged.

- Don't insist on reading the story if a child just wants to look at pictures. You don't have to read all the words and you can even use your own words.

- Remember the goal is to have a positive experience.

And, by the way, you're never too old to enjoy hearing a book read. Do include older children in reading activities. You can make it a family activity. My husband, Sam, has rich memories of family gathered after supper to read from the Bible, reciting memory verses with discussion. Those experiences continue to sustain and motivate him to share out loud portions of his current reading material to stimulate our conversation.

What to Read to Children

Books are a gift you can open again and again. With books you can introduce children to the world of ideas, to their heritage or other cultures. Reading can expand children's minds to include new people, faraway places and exotic animals, as well as allow them to explore their feelings through topics familiar to them.

We can convey our own interests, values and cultural heritage to our children and grandchildren by our choice of reading material. A book helps us to express ourselves and is a lasting gift.

I have chosen some of my favorites for you, listed by age. But there are so many to choose from and so many new ones coming out all the time, I recommend consulting a knowledgeable librarian or a helpful children's bookstore employee who can guide you in making appropriate selections. The Essential Grandparent Reading Circle will also make suggestions. There are some excellent catalogs for books listed in Resources for Grandparents. Books that were your children's or your own favorites will be especially enjoyed by both parent and child. Choosing topics that interest you promotes common interests.

Reading to a child is a perfect activity to help fulfill the five promises General Colin Powell's America's Promise has made to our nation's youth. Reading is a vehicle for providing the five promises which children need: mentoring, protecting, nurturing, preparing and inspiring to give service.

Don't overlook the bargains you can find at used bookstores and garage sales. I've also discovered some interesting old, out-of-print books in antique stores. I collect books to keep on hand as ever-ready gifts for my favorite young readers.

Books on tape are another way to keep children interested when an adult isn't available. One of the best gifts for any age, including newborns, is a cassette player. Then you can continue to give tapes and be associated with this activity, almost as if you were a participant. In fact, a cassette tape of you reading a book, telling a story or singing is a great way for your grandchild to keep you close.

Books for the whole family, such as picture books on nature, art, history or science, are a catalyst for family togetherness. Encyclopedias, dictionaries, an atlas and other reference books are important additions to a family's library. Nowadays when I read to a child, I find myself recapturing the fond moments of reading to my own children and even some of the magic of my childhood when, sitting close, my mother, father or my Aunt Della read to me. If there isn't a child at hand, find a kid and read to him. Try it. The life you change may also be your own.

Books are useful tools for coping with feelings and emotions. They broaden a kid's understanding of the world. When confronted by the loss of a pet, the whole family can find comfort with *The Tenth Best Thing About Barney* (Judith Viorst, Alladin Books, 1976) or

My favorite book of childhood, The Story About Ping, *is currently in print. I delight in giving it to children and telling them how I loved it when I was their age.*

Beyond the Ridge (Paul Goble, Alladin Books, 1989); *Molly's Pilgrim* (Barbara Cohen, A Bantam First Skylark, 1990) teaches about differences; and *Chicken Sunday* (Patricia Polacco, Philomel Books, 1992) celebrates cultural diversity and intergenerational relationships. *Brother Eagle, Sister Sky: A Message from Chief Seattle* (Susan Jeffers, Dial Books, 1991) and, for older children, *The Education of Little Tree* (Forest Carter, University of New Mexico Press, 1990) touch our hearts with the Native American reverence for nature. *Minou* (Mindy Bingham, Advocacy Press, 1987) sends a positive message for girls to become strong and self-reliant.

Books are not the only available reading material. Newspapers, magazines, comic books or whatever is handy can be used. Get children interested in current events through the newspaper or having fun with comics and cartoons. Stimulate interests with books that expand on their current hobbies or sports. Or try to influence them with books that interest you. Reading books that your own kids loved when they were young provides a great connection across generations. Kids love to hear about when their parents were young.

Because there are so many books to choose from, old and new, use the following selections as a resource to guide your reading and gift choices.

BIRTH TO EIGHTEEN MONTHS

Board books of everyday items or animals.

Brown, Margaret Wise. *Goodnight Moon.* New York: Harper-Collins, 1947.

———. *The Runaway Bunny.* New York: HarperCollins, 1942.

Carl, Eric. *The Very Hungry Caterpillar.* New York: Putnam, 1981.

Carter, David A. *How Many Bugs in a Box.* New York: Simon & Schuster, 1988.

Dyer, Jane. *Moo, Moo, Peek a Boo.* New York: Random House, 1986

Frasier, Debra. *On the Day You Were Born.* New York: Harcourt, Brace & Co., 1995.

Hill, Eric. *Where's Spot.* New York: Putnam, 1981.

Kunhardt, Dorothy. *Pat the Bunny.* Racine, Wis.: Western Publishing, 1942.

Mother Goose. New York: Scholastic, 1968.

Scarry, Richard. *Cars and Trucks and Things That Go.* New York: Golden Press, 1976.

EIGHTEEN MONTHS TO THREE YEARS

Barton, Byron. *Machines At Work.* New York: Harper-Collins, 1987.

Day, Alexandra. *Good Dog Carl.* San Diego: Green Tiger Press, 1985.

Eastman, Philip D. *Are You My Mother?* Seattle: Beginner Books, 1960.

Freeman, Don. *Corderoy.* New York: Viking, 1968.

Gomi, Taro. *Everyone Poops.* Brooklyn, N.Y.: Kane/Miller Book Publishers, 1993.

Martin, Bill Jr., and John Archambault. *Chicka Chicka Boom Boom.* New York: Simon & Schuster, 1989.

McCloskey, Robert. *Make Way for Ducklings.* New York: Viking, 1941.

Numeroff, Laura. *If You Give a Mouse a Cookie.* New York: HarperCollins, 1985.

Potter, Beatrix. *The Tale of Peter Rabbit and His Friends.* New York: Crown, 1900.

Rey, H. A. *Curious George.* Boston: Houghton-Mifflin, 1941.

Seuss, Dr. *Green Eggs and Ham.* New York: Random House, 1960.

Slobodkina, Esphyr. *Caps for Sale.* New York: HarperCollins, 1947.

Waddell, Martin. *Can't You Sleep Little Bear?* New York: HarperCollins, 1992.

————. *Owl Babies.* Cambridge, Mass.: Candlewick Press, 1992.

Zelinsky, Paul. *Wheels on the Bus.* New York: Penguin, 1990.

THREE YEARS TO SIX YEARS

Bingham, Mindy. *Minou.* Santa Barbara: Advocacy Press, 1987.

Burton, Virginia Lee. *Mike Mulligan and His Steam Shovel.* Boston: Houghton-Mifflin, 1939.

Dahl, Roald. *James & the Giant Peach.* New York: Penguin, 1961.

Flack, Marjorie. *Angus and the Ducks.* New York: Doubleday, 1978.

Flack, Marjorie and Kurt Wiese. *The Story About Ping.* New York: Puffin Books, 1933.

Fulton, Janet. *The Raggedy Ann Book.* New York: Golden Press, 1969.

Goble, Paul. *Beyond the Ridge.* New York: Alladin Books, 1989.

Gruelle, Johnny. *More Raggedy Ann and Andy Stories*. New York: Bobbs-Merrill, 1977.

Hanford, Martin. *Where's Waldo*. New York: Little, Brown, 1987.

Johnson, Crockett. *Harold and the Purple Crayon*. New York: Harper & Row, 1955.

Lamorisse, Albert. *The Red Balloon*. New York: Doubleday, 1978.

Leaf, Munroe. *The Story of Ferdinand*. New York: Puffin Books, 1977.

Lindgren, Astrid. *Pippi Longstocking*. New York: Viking, 1950.

McClosky, Robert. *Blueberries for Sal*. Boston: Houghton-Mifflin, 1948.

Mosel, Arlene. *Tikki Tikki Tembo*. New York: Henry Holt & Co., 1968.

Parish, Peggy. *Amelia Bedelia*. New York: HarperCollins, 1992.

Piper, Wally. *The Little Engine That Could*. New York: Putnam, 1926.

Rosentheil, Agnes. *Mimi Takes Charge*. Santa Barbara: Advocacy Press, 1991.

Seuss, Dr. *Cat in the Hat*. New York: Random House, 1957.

Viorst, Judith. *Alexander and the Terrible, Horrible, No Good, Very Bad Day*. New York: Aladdin, 1972.

———. *The Tenth Best Thing About Barney*. New York: Aladdin, 1971.

SIX TO NINE YEARS

Atwater, Richard Tupper. *Mr. Popper's Penguins*. New York: Dell, 1938.

Banks, Lynn. *Indian in the Cupboard.* New York: Avon, 1985.

Barrett, Judith. *Cloudy with a Chance of Meatballs.* New York: Macmillan, 1978.

Baylor, Byrd and Peter Parnall. *The Other Way to Listen.* New York: Charles Scribner's Sons, 1978.

Burnett, Frances. *The Secret Garden.* New York: Harper-Collins, 1969.

Carroll, Lewis. *Alice's Adventures in Wonderland.* New York: Golden Press, 1865.

Cohen, Barbara. *Molly's Pilgrim.* New York: William Morrow, 1983.

Fleischman, Sid. *Whipping Boy.* Mahwah, N.J.: Troll Assoc., 1986.

Gurney, James. *Dinotopia, the World Beneath.* Atlanta: Turner Publishing, 1995.

Jeffers, Susan. *Brother Eagle, Sister Sky.* New York: Dial Books, 1991.

Seuss, Dr. *Oh, the Places You'll Go.* New York: Random House, 1990.

Spyri, Johanna. *Heidi.* New York: Grossett & Dunlap, 1880.

Waber, Bernard. *Ira Sleeps Over.* Boston: Houghton-Mifflin, 1973.

White, E. B. *Charlotte's Web.* New York: HarperCollins, 1952.

————. *Stuart Little.* New York: HarperCollins, 1945.

NINE TO TWELVE YEARS

Babbit, Natalie. *Tuck Everlasting.* New York: Farrar, Straus & Giroux, 1985.

Blume, Judy. *Are You There God, It's Me Margaret.* New York: Dell Publishing, 1970.

Frank, Anne. *The Diary of a Young Girl.* New York: Globe Fearon, 1952.

Keene, Carolyn. *Nancy Drew Mystery Stories.* New York: Gossett & Dunlap, 1947.

L'Engle, Madeleine. *A Wrinkle in Time.* New York: Farrar, Straus & Giroux, 1962.

Lamb, Charles and Mary Lamb. *Tales from Shakespeare.* New York: Weathervane Books, 1986.

Lee, Harper. *To Kill a Mockingbird.* Reader's Digest Association, 1960.

Montgomery, Lucy Mand. *Anne of Green Gables.* New York: Crown, 1976.

Paterson, Katherine. *Bridge of Terabitha.* New York: HarperCollins, 1987.

Rawls, Wilson. *Where the Red Fern Grows.* New York: Macmillan, 1984.

Seller, Mick. *Sound, Noise and Music.* New York: Shooting Star Press, 1992.

Sewell, Anna. *Black Beauty.* New York: Farrar, Straus & Giroux, 1945.

Sperry, Armstrong. *Call It Courage.* New York: Macmillan, 1940.

Taylor, Mildred. *Friendship.* New York: Dial, 1987.

The Visual Dictionary of the Human Body. New York: Dorling Kindersley, 1991.

TEENAGERS

Avi. *True Confessions of Charlotte Doyle.* New York: Avon, 1990.

———. *Wolf Rider.* New York: HarperCollins, 1986.

Block, Francesca. *Weezie Bat.* New York: HarperCollins, 1989.

Brooks, Bruce. *Midnight Hour Encores.* New York: HarperCollins, 1986.

Campbell, Eric. *Place of Lions.* New York: Harcourt Brace, 1991.

Carter, Forrest. *The Education of Little Tree.* New York: Delacourte Press, 1986.

Lipsyte, Robert. *The Contender.* New York: HarperCollins, 1967.

Lowry, Lois. *The Giver.* Boston: Houghton-Mifflin, 1993.

Magorian, Michelle. *Good Night, Mr. Tom.* New York: HarperCollins, 1986.

Voigt, Cynthia. *Homecoming.* New York: Simon & Schuster, 1981.

This book list was compiled with the help of Maureen Carr.

11

Ask Dr. Carson

Grandparents aren't the only ones with questions about their grandparenting. Our adult children and even our grandchildren have many questions and issues concerning us. Family relationships are complicated and fraught with dilemmas. The family is our training ground. Learning to get along with family members teaches us how to get along in the world. It may seem to be a paradox, but I find that it's often the more caring families who come to me with their problems, the ones who are open to looking at themselves and working things out. I chose these questions because they are representative of the many I receive.

Q: *My husband doesn't take the initiative when it comes to making plans with the grandchildren and family. He does go along with my plans without complaint, but I wish he'd get more involved and not leave it all up to me. It makes me wonder if he cares. Besides, it would be more fun to share the planning. Do you have any ideas?*

A: There are two points to consider. First, is this a long-standing pattern? What was his participation when your children were young? In other words, is this the way it's always been? If his passivity is well-established, change now is less likely. Second, take an honest look at yourself and ask: Is there any way you may be discouraging his participation by criticizing, complaining or overriding his suggestions?

Many fathers and grandfathers have been systematically trained out of parenting by wives who tend to maintain the executive position with children and family, even when they say they'd love to relinquish it. They are fearful that the father won't "do it right." This criticism may be due to an unwillingness to accept the father's parenting style or to help him learn. Certainly it squelches his initiative. These fathers and grandfathers give up and wait for instructions.

Involve your husband when you're making plans by seeking his input—his thoughts and ideas. That is a way to share the planning and get feedback on his interests. Be careful not to put down his ideas. It's doubtful he'd be such a willing participant if he weren't deriving pleasure from going along with your plans. Encourage his participation by engaging him and the grandchildren in activities he really enjoys or can teach. Reading to the children is another good vehicle for involvement.

Your question brings to mind the saying, "Lead, follow or get out of the way." Your husband is happily following your lead, and no one is in your way. Take pleasure in that.

Q: *I've got to get my life back. Help me to say, "No," to requests for baby-sitting. When I refuse, I feel that I'm not living up to my grandparent role. I even feel guilty for not offering my services when they don't ask, because I know my kids are stressed and would benefit from some free time.*

A: Baby-sitting is not a requirement of grandparenting. Not only are you entitled to your own life, but it is important not to burden your children by making them your life. It sounds as though you need a reminder that you are not responsible for the lives your adult children have chosen. You can ease their burdens, but you can't remove them, nor should you expect to.

You will provide enthusiasm for life by your example of actively pursuing your own friends and activities. Not only does this make you a more positive and interesting person, but it also gives you the energy to help out willingly. On the other hand, when you feel put upon, you become frustrated, and that creates tensions—just the opposite of what you want.

As with money withdrawn from the bank, your energy must be replenished regularly, or you will be in danger of becoming emotionally overdrawn. It is painful to see your children struggle, and they do need all the help you can offer. Each grandparent must find her own *happy medium* of how much she can give. It's a juggle that will vary according to your needs and theirs, but it does mean it's okay to say no.

At the other extreme is a grandmother I know who announced at the birth of her first grandchild, "I will not babysit." She set out her intentions up-front. It strikes me as sad; I know it disappointed her kids, but by stating her intentions up-front, at least her position was clear.

Q: *My mother lives three thousand miles away and visits occasionally. It is so disappointing that she takes so little interest in our delightful six-year-old daughter, Melissa. On her last visit, after spending a short time with her granddaughter, she wanted to spend her time at the mall. (She lives near New York City, so it's not as though shopping is a novelty.) My encouragement of, "Mom, you can shop anytime, but Melissa would really like to spend time getting to know her grandma," fell on deaf ears. Her indifference seems unnatural and is a real loss for all of us. It breaks my heart that I'm unable to share my joy of fatherhood with my mother.*

A: Your disappointment is understandable. Remember the old adage, "You can lead a horse to water but you can't make him drink"? It's sad but true, and, in this case, a loss for all. Beyond encouraging the grandparent-granddaughter relationship by letting your mother know how important it is to the whole family, you can continue to promote it by keeping in touch by phone and through letters from you and Melissa, perhaps sending her Melissa's drawings and photos. There's nothing more you can do to make it happen. Some grandparents just aren't interested.

This is probably a painful reminder of your own childhood disappointments with your mother. Hoping that she might do the things with your child that she wasn't able to do with you is a way you seek to make up for the past by finally sharing a longed-for closeness with your mother. Accept this unhappy reality, but keep the doors open. Bridge your family's intergenerational void by cultivating surrogate grandparents. Invite some grandparent-types to your home for a meal or to share an outing. There are many older people who would welcome the opportunity to share the warmth of your family.

Q: *Our daughter-in-law's parents are in a financial position to give our children and grandchildren much more than we can. They are generous and always sending "big" presents to the grandchildren. We just can't compete. We feel overshadowed and inadequate. We give what we can, but it's never as spectacular, nor does it create the same excitement.*

A: The key is your feeling of competition. Your attitude may be the problem. The way you define a problem determines what it becomes. Why compete? Why compare? Thoughtfulness and caring are the building blocks of real, caring relationships. It's nice that your grandchildren have generous grandparents, but remember that the amount of money spent on a gift does not measure its worth. Get creative in your gift giving. There are so many ways to give that will build relationships. [See chapter 9, The Joys of Giving.]

The value of grandparents is not measured by their material gifts alone but by the experiences they provide, the possibilities they open, the philosophy and heritage they hand down, and their love for and belief in their grandchild's worth. Don't lose sight of the most meaningful and lasting gift of all, the one money can't buy: giving of yourself.

Q: *Our family is quite diverse, and as a result, family gatherings are often fraught with tension. Discussions invariably deteriorate into arguments, and Uncle Oliver always drinks too much. We sure fall short of the ideal family, and I worry that this can't be healthy for the grandchildren. I just dread the holidays.*

A: Family is the training ground for learning to get along in the world, so diversity in family, whatever it may be— racial, religious, cultural, political or personality—gives us a chance to learn how to get along with others. Since families are made up of people, each invariably has its share of bores, opinionated types, complainers, lushes or just plain difficult people. In order to make our way in life, we need to learn how to get along with all kinds of people we may not choose to be with, like teachers, co-workers and bosses. Parents and grandparents can lead the way by their example of acceptance and by finding ways to minimize the negative impact. Plan some communal activities that everyone can enjoy together, such as singing or responsive reading or, perhaps, going around the table to tell what each person is thankful for this Thanksgiving or hopes for in the coming New Year. Ceremonies that relate to your heritage also provide positive group experiences.

Problems and rivalries in families are the reality that shatters the myth of the picture-perfect family of our dreams. Your attitude toward these gatherings, your own ability to accept difficulty, will teach valuable lessons to your children and grandchildren. It's a funny thing, but in time of need it's often those difficult family members who come forward with support and understanding. Sometimes those with problems are more responsive to the problems of others. They know what it's like to have problems.

Q: *I'm uncomfortable with the expectation that my children must always be expected to kiss their grandparents hello and goodbye. This is even extended to other visitors who are present. My kids hate this requirement, and I think it's unhealthy. How do I handle this without offending anyone?*

A: You are right. The demand for children to show affection on command is not fair to them. It teaches them to bypass their own feelings and act out what others want from them. This removes them from their own feelings. Stop and think about the message we are sending to children when we tell them to deny their own feelings. Saying things like, "Now that didn't hurt, did it?" after receiving a shot from the doctor is really confusing. The child is being told to disbelieve what she felt. After all, it really did hurt. It creates a vague sense that real feelings are not acceptable, maybe even bad. Social consideration requires a verbal hello and goodbye or goodnight, but kisses are not required. Tell your children in advance that a greeting is enough. This gives them permission to resist obligatory kisses. Encourage them to verbally express their positive feelings. When they are asked, "Where's my kiss?" support them by intervening with a statement that helps to smooth things over. Something like, "Say hello to Grandma," or, "Sammy doesn't feel like kissing just now." Children should not be forced to show affection.

Q: *All the grandchildren shun my father because he's too strict. I don't want my son to be deprived of a relationship with his grandpa. I'd like him to learn to accept him even though he's a rigid person. But how do I do it?*

A: Your son's life will be enriched by developing a relationship with his grandfather. Much depends on your attitude and acceptance of him. Children follow their parents' lead. Encourage their relationship by helping your son understand that "that's just Grandpa's way." Point out Grandpa's good qualities and tell stories about how you managed to get along with him. Promote activities they might enjoy together so that they can develop common interests. Good luck! It will be a gift to both of them.

Q: *My daughter told the good news that she was expecting her first child to my mother before she told me. It really hurt to discover I was to become a grandmother from my mother instead of my daughter. I know my relationship with my daughter and my mom hasn't been smooth. We have had our problems. My daughter and mother have such a close relationship I have often felt left out, but this is the greatest blow of all. Will I be robbed of the joys of my grandparenthood? I don't want to make matters worse by confrontation, but I can't ignore the way I feel.*

A: You are fortunate that your mother and daughter have such a special relationship. Theirs is a perfect example of that special bond between grandparent and grandchild. It is nurturing and healthy for them to share their lives. It really isn't taking anything away from you. It is a reminder to you that you don't have the relationship you'd hope for with your daughter. You will now have an opportunity to develop the warm and loving relationship you long for with your own grandchild. As your daughter becomes a mother herself, she will need your love and encouragement. Just keep loving her and hope she forgives you for the times you disappoint her. We all disappoint our children in one way or another. Focus on the grandparent you plan to become.

Q: *I know you advise grandparents not to criticize their children's parenting, but my husband and I are worried sick and feel we should speak out. We witnessed our daughter, Peggy, shake her four-month-old baby very hard. The baby cries a lot, and Peggy is pretty frazzled. This is her first child, and it all seems to be very hard for her. She seems to be losing her self-control, and we're afraid she'll do it again.*

A: Your concern is well-founded. There are times when grand-
    parents should be advocates for their grandchildren and
    speak up, regardless of the consequences. Your daughter is
    evidently overwhelmed by the demands of motherhood
    and needs help. There are several things to consider. She
    may be experiencing post-partum depression, in which case
    her doctor should be consulted. Are she and her husband
    having problems? Most marriages undergo a major adjust-
    ment with the arrival of a child, especially the first one.
    New parents may easily feel separated from each other.
    Perhaps they need some time together. Is Peggy on any
    medication or drugs that might be affecting her moods?

Find a neutral time, when things are calm, to talk to her
frankly. Avoid accusations. Parents who abuse their children suffer from guilt and feelings of inadequacy. Criticism will make her
defensive and only make matters worse. Voice your concern and
willingness to help. Ask what you can do to make it easier for her.
Can you provide some relief so that she can have a break? Bring
her husband into the discussion. There are groups that help parents in trouble.

Also, the baby should be checked by a pediatrician. Because a
baby's brain is not fully developed, shaking can cause damage.

Suggest these steps when she feels she's losing it:

1. Take a deep breath; it helps to control frustration.

2. Count to ten.

3. Call you or a friend.

4. Tell the pediatrician.

You are right; this is definitely a special situation that begs for
grandparent involvement.

Epilogue

After All Is Said and Done . . .

"We're all of us tiny drops in a vast ocean, but some sparkle and sparkle."
CAMELOT

We must each find our own answer to the question, *"What is worth doing?"* as we become more conscious of the present moment dropping through the hourglass. What will be most rewarding and yield the highest rate of enrichment to our lives? How will our legacy to family measure our lives?

I hope that this book has informed and encouraged your choice, for I fervently believe that active and involved grandparenting holds a key to our health and that of our children and grandchildren. Though I am wary of simple answers to such complex questions, I am convinced by my own studies and the research of others, my patients and the many people of all ages who I have interviewed, that this is true.

Because grandparenting changes from generation to generation, involvement pushes us to be adventurous and creative. By keeping in touch with younger generations, we are stretched to remain open to learning which, in turn, allows us to grow and live our lives to the fullest. We are never grown up once and for all. The life cycle continually presents us with

*Get something that will get
you out of bed.*

GEORGE BURNS
advice upon turning 100

new tasks and challenges. When we accept them, we remain vital and energized. What's in it for us? Purpose, meaning, health, joy and pure delight, relationship, love, many happy surprises. The list goes on and on. . . .

When giving of ourselves we can strive to achieve inter-generational equity by redistributing our accumulated assets: our knowledge and philosophy gathered over years of experience that

*The number of centenarians
in the U.S. has doubled every
decade since 1970. It will
cause us to rethink their meaning for society and our ideas
about age. We're approaching
the day when to be seventy or
eighty is going to be middle-
aged.*

CARYL STERN,
Parade Magazine

combines to become our wisdom and our material goods. The equity value is deeply rooted in our culture as an ethical and moral value. It is evident in our Constitution and in the Bill of Rights. Our spiritual and religious traditions frame this concept as service: giving generously of ourselves and our possessions.

It is by embracing this notion of giving back to others that we do much of society's most important work: caring for children and aging

parents, providing emotional and financial stability for the family, and passing on values and tradition. These contributions tend to be invisible and unmeasured by conventional economics, yet we grandparents provide the nation's social glue. It is important to recognize that a golden age of completely carefree living evades us. We cannot escape our responsibilities to others.

Research has shown that people who do the best job facing

*Whatsoever a man soweth,
that shall he also reap.*

2 COR. 6:7

life's challenges perceive three things about themselves: They believe: (1) that they are capable; (2) that their lives have meaning; and (3) that they have control in what happens in their lives.

They also possess these four skills: (1) self-discipline; (2) the ability to work with other people; (3) personal responsibility; and (4) good judgment. Our task is to supply our grandchildren with the building blocks for these beliefs and skills by sharing our time, wisdom and resources.

It is easy to mistakenly believe that today's children are maturing earlier than children in the past, and to feel that our input is unnecessary. This is far from true. In reality, although they are exposed to things that used to be morally unthinkable—drugs, sex, guns and violence—which may make them more sophisticated about the world, there is no real maturity. These children do not possess the skills to deal with the challenges they face. In fact, they are overwhelmed, confused and frightened by them and, too often, on their own to decipher the competing messages that bombard them daily.

Trot your own horse. Don't get in the same rut as everyone else.

Advice to little Barbara Jordan by her grandfather

Children are our future. We have much to tell each other. We offer a promise of hope to each other. Our mutual needs bring us full circle on the cycle of life. Just look around, pick up a newspaper, turn on the television, speak to a teacher or, better yet, to a child. It is evident that we must extend ourselves to embrace and advocate for all children. There is no such thing as somebody else's grandchildren. Our efforts must include caring about the condition of our planet and the social order. We would do well to adopt the Native American tradition that mandates considering the consequences of our actions today upon seven future generations. Because the task is enormous there are many choices, many paths to making a difference. Don't be discouraged by the knowledge that you can not possibly do it all, but begin with a full measure of energy and love. Choose life and travel toward the sun.

Children inherit not only the legacies that their elders impart but also the void that is left by what they withhold.

Grandparents, never doubt it: *You are essential!*

**Please send your thoughts and stories to
Dr. Lillian Carson, 1187 Coast Village Rd.,
Suite 1-316, Montecito, CA 93108-1725
Fax: (805) 565-1049
Email: *drlcarson@aol.com*
Web site: *www.essentialgrandparent.com***

Resources for Grandparents

Toys and Gifts

Not only have these catalogs provided some happy answers to my search for quality, creative toys and gifts for my grandchildren, they have proved to be time-savers as well.

ANIMAL TOWN CATALOG
   Nurturing children, family and environment through cooperation; cooperative and noncompetitive games; outdoor playthings; environmental board games; children's tapes, books and puzzles; books on cooperation and family activities. 800-445-8642

BACK TO BASIC TOYS CATALOG
   Toys, games and hobbies. 800-356-5360

BIO-BOTTOMS CATALOG
   Clothing. 800-766-1254

BRIO
   Infant to eight years and more.
   Well-constructed toys that encourage imaginative play.
   800-558-6863

Chinaberry Catalog
Books and other treasures for the entire family.
800-776-2242, Mon-Sat 6-6, PST

Gifts for Grandkids
1-888-472-6354

Hanna Anderson Catalog
Quality Swedish clothing, 100 percent cotton.
800-222-0544

HearthSong Catalog
Crafts, things-to-do. Environmentally correct.
800-325-2502, 24 hours, 7 days
outside USA and Canada, 1-707-829-1550

Kar-Ben Copies: A Growing Jewish Library for
Young Children
For catalog, 800-452-7236

Lakeshore Learning Materials Catalog
Furniture, learning materials, toys and school supplies
for infants, preschool, elementary and special education.
800-421-5354

Lilly's Kids Catalog
Toys.
800-430-5555, 24 hours, 7 days

Music for Little People Catalog
Audio, video, musical instruments and more.
800-727-2233, 24 hours, 7 days

This Country's Toys Catalog
Toys with long-term play value, made in the USA.
800-359-1233

Young and Creative Catalog
Crafts, art, music, world cultures crafts.
800-609-8697

Zillions: Consumer Reports for Kids
Magazine for ages eight to 14. 800-234-2078

Reading for Grandparents on Parenting

Here are a few books and magazines I've found to keep me current on parenting practices in the 1990s.

Books

Ames, Louise Bates and Frances L. Ilg. *Your One-Year-Old.* New York: Dell, 1982. This is the first in a series of books for each year of childhood, concluding with *Your Ten-to-Fourteen-Year-Old.* These books provide information on expectable development that is useful and reassuring. I give them to parents on their kid's birthday.

Beyond the Pink and Blue Predicament. Girls Incorporated, National Resource Center, 411 W. Michigan St., Indianapolis, IN 46202. 317-634-7546.

Bingham, Mindy and Sandy Stryker. *Things Will Be Different for My Daughter.* New York: Penguin Books, 1995.

Brazelton, T. Berry. *Touchpoints.* Boston: Addison-Wesley, 1992.

Coloroso, Barbara. *Kids Are Worth It! Giving Your Child Inner Discipline.* New York: Avon, 1994.

Edelman, Marian Wright. *The Measure of Our Success: A Letter to My Children and Yours.* Boston: Beacon Press, 1992.

Godfrey, Joline. *No More Frogs to Kiss: 99 Ways to Give Economic Power to Girls.* New York: Harper Business, 1995.

Rosemond, John. *John Rosemond's 6-Point Plan for Raising Happy, Healthy Children.* Kansas City, Mo.: Andrews & McMeel, 1991.

Sale, June and Kit Kollenberg with Ellen Melinkoff. *The Working Parents Handbook.* New York: Fireside, 1996.

Short-Changing Girls, Short-Changing America. Washington, D.C.: American Association of University Women, 1991. 800-225-9998.

Solter, Aletha. *The Aware Baby.* Goleta, Calif.: Shining Star Press, 1992. 805-968-1868.

Trelease, Jim. *The Read-Aloud Handbook.* New York: Penguin Books, 1995.

Magazines

Child Magazine, P.O. Box 3176, Harlan, IA 51593-0367.

Mothering Magazine, Subscription office: P.O. Box 532, Mt. Morris, IL 61054. 800-424-3308.

Parents Magazine, P.O. Box 3055, Harlan, IA 51593-4119. 800-361-8057.

Parents Magazine Expert Advice Line: 900-680-KIDS (costs 95 cents per minute).

Music and Reading for Children

Lipson, Eden Ross. *The New York Times Parent's Guide to the Best Books for Children.* New York: Random House, 1988. (Lipson is the Children's Editor of the *New York Times.*)

Sale, Laurie. *Growing Up with Music: A Guide to the Best Recorded Music for Children.* New York: Avon Books, 1992.

Trelease, Jim. *The Read-Aloud Handbook.* New York: Penguin Books, 1995.

Just for Grandparents

Here are some publications that address the needs of grandparents along with a few readings that have enlightened my travels through the life cycle.

Angelou, Maya. *On the Pulse of Morning.* New York: Random House, 1993.

Callanan, Maggie and Patricia Kelley. *Final Gifts.* New York: Bantam, 1993.

Canfield, Jack and Mark Victor Hansen. *Chicken Soup for the Soul.* Deerfield Beach, Fla.: Health Communications, Inc., 1993.

Carter, Jimmy. *The Virtues of Aging.* New York: Ballantine, 1998.

Condon, Gerald M. and Jeffrey L. Condon. *Beyond the Grave: The Right and the Wrong Way of Leaving Money to Your Children (and Others).* New York: Harper Business, 1995.

Craven, Margaret. *I Heard the Owl Call My Name.* New York: Doubleday, 1973.

Downes, Peggy, Ilene Tuttle, Patricia and Viginia Mudd. *The New Older Woman.* Berkeley: Celestial Arts, 1996.

Friedan, Betty. *The Fountain of Age.* New York: Simon & Schuster, 1993.

Lindbergh, Anne Morrow. *Gift from the Sea.* New York: Random House, 1986.

Sheehy, Gail. *New Passages: Mapping Your Life Across Time.* New York: Random House, 1992.

———. *The Silent Passage: Menopause.* New York: Random House, 1992.

Viorst, Judith. *Necessary Losses.* New York: Fawcett Gold Medal, 1986.

Wellness Letter. University of California at Berkeley. Subscription Department: P.O. Box 420163, Palm Coast, FL 32142.

Getting Support and Getting Involved

AARP Grandparent Information Center provides information and resources to help people who have become primary caregivers for their grandchildren. For information: AARP Information Center, Box MM, 601 E Street NW, Washington, D.C. 20049.

America's Promise, The Alliance for Youth. A national organization led by General Colin Powell, dedicated to mobilizing the nation to ensure our children and youth have access to the fundamental resources they need to become successful adults. To become mentor or tutor call 888-559-6884.

Center for Media Literacy. For catalogue on critical viewing: 800-226-9494.

Ellis Island Foundation, Wall of Honor Museum of Ellis Island open 9:30 A.M. to 5 P.M., 7 days; take Statue of Liberty/Ellis Island Ferry from Battery Park. For information: 212-883-1986.

Foster Grandparents Program. To find a branch near you: 202-606-5000, ext. 199.

Generations United. A National Coalition on Intergenerational Issues and Programs c/o CWLA, 440 First Street, N.W., Suite 310, Washington, D.C. 20001-2085. 202-638-2952.

Grandparents of the '90s. Support for grandparents raising their grandchildren. For assistance in finding or starting a support group: 508-672-7645.

Grandtravel. For grandparents who are searching for creative (but pricey) ways to strengthen ties with their grandchildren: 6900 Wisconsin Avenue, Suite 706, Chevy Chase, Maryland 20815.

Gray Panthers. People of all ages working toward common ground and solutions to today's problems. P.O. Box 21477 Washington, D.C. 20009; 800-280-5362.

Intergenerational Program. On Lok Senior Health Service and Wu Yee Children's Services, San Francisco, California, promotes intergenerational activities. Call 415-292-8888 for information about this type of program.

Modern Maturity Magazine, American Association of Retired Persons. For AARP Membership: P.O. Box 199, Long Beach, California 90801.

National Storytelling Association. For catalog of books or membership: P.O. Box 309, Jonesborough, Tennessee 37659, or: 800-525-4514.

Phone Home. Be a phone friend to a "latchkey" kid. There are 10 million children home alone after school. Forty-two percent are between five and nine years. To join or start your own chapter call 213-520-5000.

A Piece of Blue Sky, The Cult Awareness Network. For information: 312-267-7777.

Index

Help the Kids You Love, Love Books

"If you read to a child 20 minutes a day, that child will hear 1 million additional words a year and will gain 1,000 additional vocabulary words."
—Delaine Easton, California State Superintendent of Schools

"Young children who are regularly and lovingly read to have a priceless advantage from the start. Every child deserves someone to share a book with, and what a wonderful 'someone' a grandparent is."
—Patricia S. Schroeder, President and CEO, Association of American Publishers

Join Dr. Lillian Carson's
Essential Grandparent™
Reading Circle
for Grandparents & Others
WHY + HOW + WHAT to read to kids

The life you change may be your own!

- -

Mail to: Dr. Lillian Carson, The Essential Grandparent Reading Circle
1187 Coast Village Road, Suite 1-316
Montecito, CA 93108-1725
FAX (805) 565-1049   email *drlcarson@aol.com*

Yes, I want to change a child's life by becoming a reader. Enroll me in The Essential Grandparent Reading Circle and send my free newsletter. I understand there is absolutely no cost or obligation.

Name _____ Ages of kids _____

Mailing Address _____
Please Print Legibly   Street   City   State   Zip Code

The ABC's of parenting

The two women who help Hollywood's A-list get their ZZZs share their no-fail, family friendly solution that will get any baby, toddler or preschooler to sleep.

Code #5601 • $14.95

Code #5466 • $14.95

Noted psychologist Ann Dunnewold offers you a way out of the Perfect Parenting race without sacrificing yourself or your family.